JOSH BROWN

Memoir

Stories From Under The Truck To Red Carpet's Fame

Sandi Hall

TABLE OF CONTENTS

TABLE OF CONTENTS

    CHAPTER 1
    GROUND ZERO

    CHAPTER 2
    SURVIVAL OF THE FITTEST

    CHAPTER 3
    THROUGH THE GLASS, DARKLY

    CHAPTER 4
    A LAND OF MISFITS

    CHAPTER 5
    THROUGH THE DUST

    CHAPTER 6
    BENEATH THE CANOPY

    CHAPTER 7
    SCREAMS IN THE HIGHLANDS

    CHAPTER 8
    THE HORSE'S MANE

    CHAPTER 9
    TALES FROM LOWER EAST SIDE

    CHAPTER 10
    THE FOREST OF MY OWN CONSTRUCTION

CHAPTER 1
GROUND ZERO

I was born to drink. I was birthed to drink. My mother drank the same way I did. I was raised to be a man and drink like the male version of my mother.

There was no discussion about the spiritual nature of things. No mention of God. Our universe revolved around country-western, outlaw, eighteen-wheeler culture, and that was it. My mother had a covert relationship with a trucker for approximately eight years. My father feared her, so he usually avoided her. Because the trucker was frequently away, I became the man of the house: a responsibility that some may have found unsuitable, but fuck it, what else was there to do? She was everything I had.

AJ Spurs was known as The Iron Horse. It was a country tavern and restaurant. If she was home, that was the gathering spot. That was Ground Zero. It's where all the chaos happened. That, and Boozie's. Boozie's hasn't been around for a while. AJ Spurs lasted till recently.

The biggest cowboys and truckers would drink in there, and my mother and I would watch from the sidelines, she in her torn jean jacket and permed blond hair, and me in my Levis and shitkickers. My mother would always, and very unexpectedly, say, "Hey! Why do you have that comb in your back pocket?" The guy with the comb in his back pocket must have been three hundred pounds of muscle, lard, and cowboy hat, and he spun around, not believing for a moment that he had heard the question correctly, and said, "I'm sorry, ma'am?" She tried again: "You heard me: That comb in your back pocket, it looks faggy."

What the fuck is happening? I put on a strong look, but within, I was shitting my pants.

We're dead. I'm eight or nine at this point, and we're done.

Before I knew it, they'd be buying her complimentary Calypso Coffees, which she'd order with light rum, Tia Maria, coffee, and a dollop of whipped cream on top—basically a speedball. She had won them over with charm, character, grit, and something else that none of us could quite put our finger on.

Then the night began, one of seemingly thousands.

I'd sneak away for a beer now and then, but I was on guard. I needed to make sure we'd be home by sunup.

Years later, one night in the same location, her new lover wound up under the vehicle. We conducted a drinking contest at his request. "You don't want to do that," my mother advised him, but he persisted. After around fifteen drinks, he vanished, too inebriated to return to the table after a trip to the restroom. The owner, whom I'd known since I was a child, had come in from stacking fruit outdoors and informed us that he had noticed his legs poking out from beneath his vehicle and had passed out. "You don't fuck with us," I heard my mother say under her breath, with a smile that only suggested victory. That similar smile crawled across her face the first time she came to see me in juvenile jail. It was an expression she wore as effortlessly as her makeup every morning, yet it was not something she could remove.

You can play, but don't expect to walk out unhurt and self-confident.

1968

MY FATHER OFTEN TELLS THE STORY OF THE DAY I WAS BORN. Men were not permitted to enter the rooms where women were giving birth. This was not the case at the time. They arrived after the fact: "We sat in the waiting room or at home. We became taxis after the water broke. That's how things were then.

My mother had me for an hour and a half, from beginning to end. My brother, there was less time. "She was the type of person who just wanted to move on to the next step or party."The doctor finally called me in, wearing a large, twisted smile. I'd been listening to her scream louder than everyone else in the hospital, as had all of the expectant fathers. She continued yelling, 'Get this FUCKING THING OUTTA ME!!!' Going in there wasn't my first thought, but the doctor brought me in anyway, and there you were, all bleeding and bruised, with your head horribly deformed, like a cone. It appeared that someone had seized and stretched it till it resembled an eggplant rather than a head. It was half as long as my arm. I said, 'Put it back!'"

He always ends with a huge, exaggerated belly laugh.

I know he thinks the story is like telling me that the first time he saw me was one of the greatest moments in his life—this newborn miracle, this reveal of a consummated love—but it always sounds like he's showing his buddies a turd after a traumatic shit that clogged up the toilet and not even liquid Drano could clear it.

1979

First time I went to a drive-in. I had a beer in the back seat of a rusted sky-blue Oldsmobile. The smell inside was of upholstery cleaner, warm lager, and stale cigarettes. My best friend Danny's uncle was the driver. Danny had Scotch tape wrapped across the right side of his black glasses. His eyes were permanently slanted due to the number of procedures he had on them as a child. Danny, although being three years older than me, was my best buddy, yet he loathed me. I mean, he loved me as much as we all loved each other, given that your nearest neighbor was at least a mile away, but there was always something extra about me that stabbed at him: maybe my father was an actor, or that I was given a motorcycle long before him (at four years old), or that I didn't wear glasses. I'm not sure, but the animosity seemed to present itself more violently as time went before he committed suicide.

The film we watched that night was iconic: Bruce Lee's Game of Death. Kareem Abdul-Jabbar put a mark on Bruce Lee's chest, and the beer I endured foamed over every time I drank. I had vanilla-flavored bonbons and scarlet Twizzlers. It was a good night. There wasn't much to do out in the country—a bunch of trees, some horses, and a broken-down Yamaha YZ80—but going to the drive-in on a Friday night to hang the speaker off your half-masted window, gawking at Bruce Lee with beer in hand, and your best friend next to you sneaking looks to see how far along you were seemed like a good way to pass a slow wind's time."

Uncle what's-his-name also wore spectacles, had reddish hair pushed off to the side, and those eyes that only ex-cons have: eyes that perceived agony in everything they looked at, with clouded red whites. He didn't say much, but he smirked frequently. And the way he placed his cigarette to his lips suggested that he had seen death close up at some point, either as a grandma, a girlfriend, or while carrying out a failed dime store heist.

I left that summer, when I was eleven years old.

Danny was disturbed, but not significantly more than the rest of us. It was his father's birthday, and the entire family was present. He learned his mother was not his biological mother. He was drinking. We all drank occasionally. It was a country. But he became enraged that night. Nobody saw what was coming. He headed to his bedroom. I tried to sleep it off, maybe. But when he awoke, it remained: a reality in hell. He grabbed a .22 caliber rifle. We've all had those. It was our bucolic pride banner. He loaded it. He exited his bedroom door and turned the corner into the living room. They were all present. I'd moved away. He'd stayed. A trailer on a rural hill. His final words were, "You think I'll do it?" He bent over the rifle and pulled the trigger. He fell. His family yelled. The bullet ripped through his aorta. Blood was everywhere. He was fourteen when you could just let kids be kids. We alternated pulling each other in the red wagon around the yard. We climbed trees. We walked several miles to each other's farms. We didn't shoot ourselves; he did. He just had. In front of his entire family. They would never be the same.

I saw the uncle again the following year at Danny's funeral. He was wearing a tight blue polyester suit with white buttons and a large, pointed collar. He stepped up to the casket like the rest of us did in the scorching heat of that cinder block Mennonite church, and he stood for longer than any of us had before him. I watched him, curious as to what he was thinking, and just as I thought he was about to walk away, he brought his fingers slowly up to his lips, just as he had at the drive-in the year before, and then quickly pulled them away from his mouth with a slight, almost silent kiss that I watched fall all the way down and into that open casket, landing softly somewhere on a dead, unresponsive boy named Danny.

There was something about that man, his uncle. I'm not sure what, but it was there.

1981

HE WAS IN THE ROOM NEXT TO ME. She was upstairs. I'd heard that she awoke in the middle of the night and informed him that his foot was on her side of the bed. "What?" It was the middle of the night, but she made sure to fully awaken him to emphasize her point. "There is a longitudinal line along the center of the bed, dividing my and your sides. You stay by your side. "This is mine." She rolled over, lit a cigarette, placed it in the ashtray next to the loaded 9 millimeter pistol she kept on her bedside table, and fell asleep without ever firing it. That's the tale I heard.

He soon fell asleep in the little room next to mine. Divorce was imminent.

As I lay in my bed, I could hear him playing classical music on a battery-powered portable radio. He'd call me into his room, ask me to lie down on his bed, and then place the radio between us, turning up the volume. There were cellos, bassoons, and flutes, but it was the static that caused the greatest silent wrath in me, and I'm still astonished I didn't have an aneurysm. Punk rock seemed smoother. Punk rock evoked memories of days spent on the streets with friends, experimenting with our youth. We shaved our heads, did LSD, discovered mosh pits at night, drank warm Mexican beer, fell asleep in class, leered at cops as they drove suspiciously past, and got up at 5:00 a.m. to hop on our bikes and go surfing before the day began, even if it was flat. We wanted to continue moving. I was a teenager, and I didn't want to lie down in a depressing bed and listen to what felt like a death rites talk. I know dad had good intentions, but I was my mother's kid, and the need to relocate was instinctive.

I didn't realize until years later that happiness was his main desire. To me, happiness was always just one of many facets of who we were, but for him, it was everything. People's happiness that lasted too long terrified me, as did their inability to stop smiling. Every time I see him in my mind's eye, his smile remains constant, and everything around me falls silent.

CHAPTER 2
SURVIVAL OF THE FITTEST

1984

The Goonies

OCTOBER

I'm nervous because I've never done this before. I'm not sure who I'm dating. A car picked up me and a friend of my father's (now my guardian) and drove us to the airport. They claimed we'd be absent for a few months. I'll wash my clothes once every week. I don't have much, just a small bag. I always wind up wearing the same thing every day, so there's no point worrying about clothes. This is larger than that.

People are beginning to show up. People who support him usually surround Richard Donner, so he marches directly into Terminal Three, where we agreed to meet, with a number of his minions following behind. With a smile on his face, he commands us to line up. We do. I met Kerri when I auditioned. She's the only one, however. Dick moves down the line, pointing at each of us:

"Kerri Green: Andy; Corey Feldman: Mouth; Sean Astin: Mikey; Ke Huy Quan: Data; Jeff B. Cohen: Chunk; Martha Plimpton: Stef; and"—he places his finger in the center of my forehead—"this is who is portraying the big brat Brand. "You don't have to know his real name."

We all laugh. All of this appears to be a joke. I can't help but feel like I've done something decent for the first time in my life, but I also wonder if I'm here by mistake. I've seen several of these youngsters in previous films. It's strange that I'm here with them, taking part in it. I've never been a part of anything but situations where no one else wanted to be involved.

We land in Portland, Oregon, and then drive two hours to Astoria, a lovely seaside town with steeply pitched streets and wraparound porch homes. Corey talks the entire time, just as if he were his genuine persona, which I believe he is.

We are let out at the Thunderbird Motor Inn. After receiving our room keys, we proceed to the motel's restaurant and drop off our baggage. After dining, we all discuss whether to go bowling or to the movies. Neither of us wants to rest. We've just arrived, and the anticipation and excitement motivates us to stay up till we start shooting. We must spend as much time as possible together. We need it to feel like a family.

But we never go out; instead, we stand outside the hotel and speak.

I'm not sure what this acting industry will offer, but I admire how everyone is so excited about it. ..I do not know. ..everything.

Oregon is stunning. We're right above the harbor, and the scenery is metallic, with a faint fog hanging in the air. Old buildings and ports (Goon Docks) have a strong presence: old fishing boats tap each side of their docks, and the bridge that you can't see on the other side emits zipping sounds from the few cars and trucks going by. It's a distinct type of silence here, which I like. Any form of silence will be rare in this company.

2006

No Country for Old Men.

JUNE

Today we're flying in on a little plane over a huge and veiny terrain. I want to leap out, not because I am afraid, but because I want to be outside. My collarbone has shattered and it hurts. I broke it by ramming broadside into the car of a lady who hoped I wouldn't be there when she turned left off Highland Boulevard onto a side street near Mel's Drive In. I was rushing from one wardrobe fitting to another when she appeared out of nowhere. I felt like I was in the air forever (like this aircraft flight) and spent the time thinking about how lovely it would have been to work with the Coens and how I hoped the damage to my body wasn't too severe, given that I have children. We decided later, after the shock had worn off, to let it heal spontaneously, allowing the bone that had cracked in half to float freely until a natural calcium accumulation bonds the two jagged portions back together. The only reason I'm able to perform the film is that Llewellyn, the man I play, is shot in the right shoulder. That is the sole reason. I suppose I'm lucky.

1984

The Goonies

OCTOBER

I did my first scene with Sean (Mikey), who was a pleasure to work with. The sequence was moving and heartbreaking, but during the sixth take, we broke into uncontrollable laughter. I guess it was because I was nervous and unsure of what I was doing. You think you know what it's going to be like, but it never ends up being anything like you imagined: the feelings, the scenario, the smells, the relationships, the heat in your skull. Every moment is a discovery, an inside look at what you are made of or capable of that has never been tested before. Steven Spielberg was on set observing, and I believe he enjoyed it. He gave a small smile once. He told me to be loose. I'll remember it.

2006

No Country

JUNE

While listening to Barry Corbin's stories at the bar tonight, I noticed a gnarled hand resting on Barry's left shoulder. Barry exclaimed excitedly, then exchanged a few pleasantries with no glance at me until I decided to interject:

"Hello. "I'm Josh."

The gnarled hand's face remained expressionless as it peered at me.

"Okay . .."

"I'm playing Moss."

"Moss. Llewellyn Moss?"

"Yessir."

He looked at me for a long time, examining me.

"Josh Brolin?"

"Yessir."

"Well, I'll be damned."

"Yessir."

He continued to glance at me before returning to his conversation with Barry about nothing in particular, something about his hair. His stare reminded me of the one I used to use on my younger brother when he refused to give me something I wanted. It was a look of disdain and disgust.

I've been watching Tommy Lee Jones for so long that being there with him, being sized up by his overtly certain cowboy eyes and that Harvard something-to-prove disposition, I couldn't help but be quieter than usual and simply left to watch it all unfold right in front of me. Tommy Lee Jones. Damn. "Do you think about your clothing?" He inquired about my button-down top.

"Personal or the character's?"

(A brief pause, a glance.) "Personally."

"Yeah, I have."

A waitress walked behind us, most of her legs naked and her skirt considerably over mid thigh. He could have cared less.

"Do you know Moss is from San Saba?"

"Yessir, I do, exactly where you're from."

There was another silence, a heavy weight in the air as he peered off into the distance, as if something was there that wasn't.

"That's right."

I saw him turn and saunter out with a tiny limp, noting that there were some frat lads on the opposite side of the lobby waiting to shake his hand, but he passed right through them to the exit door and out into a dark, thin-aired Santa Fe night.

He is the best cowboy I have ever seen on film.

But when you grow up feeding sixty-five horses every morning, you develop a strong dislike for the task. Five thirty a.m. It's too early for an eight-year-old to undertake that much work.

Eventually, you learn to distinguish between people in need and those who are only there to fill an empty ego void.

But, dammit, Tommy Lee Jones. Damn.

2006

No Country

JUNE

I found a house today. It's charming, close to town, and has a small hardscape out back.

I had diarrhea all day. It was fantastic. I puked at least a dozen times. It is my favorite thing to do. I'd rather do that than work. I wonder why everyone is leaving. Javier has left, and Kelly will return to England soon. I'm not working tomorrow, so I'm hoping the stars align and I get diarrhea all day tomorrow. If I'm lucky, I might vomit a few times or have blood in my pee. One can only dream.

I miss my family and kids.

I have a mustache now. Not sure yet. Joel was concerned that it might appear that I was a member of the Village People, a flamboyant disco band from the 1970s. The collarbone is moving little less than it was before. However, the mending process is slow. It has been two and a half weeks.

Something is attempting to keep me down. I will not allow it.

1984

The Goonies

OCTOBER

Halloween.

I worked hard today and there were some excellent scenes. I was in a pleasant mood, which is becoming more common as I become accustomed to everything. After I returned to the hotel, Tony, the makeup artist, applied some cosmetics to me. I appeared to have had the shit kicked out of him. It was gruesome: blood everywhere, a fractured nose, and bulging eyes. Halloween. It was perfect. I looked terrible. The cast went to the YMCA, where the entire community turned up. Each actor sat in their own unique plastic and metal seat and signed autographs on fold-out plastic picnic tables for at least an hour, one after the other. It was a lot of fun, and I met some wonderful people, although the cosmetics I was wearing made it difficult to connect fully. Everyone else dressed funny or charming. I could have chosen the wrong costume.

I met a wonderful girl there. Her name was Keri. She had blond hair and blue eyes and was as pleasant as you would expect a blue-eyed high school blonde to be. I wonder if I'll see her again.

I miss high school. I miss all of the folks. Part of me hoped I was in that line, obtaining an autograph from someone I considered significant enough to wait in line for.

2006

No Country

JUNE

The stand-ins—Funky Will and Roy Orbison (nicknames)—are permanent fixtures on set. They remain stationary day after day. Every time I pass Will, he smiles and raises his hand in what appears to be a random gesture: half a wave, half the beginning of reaching out to shake hands but never quite doing so. Orbison, on the other hand, stands with his face fixed on the plains, one side of his lower lip hanging a little lower than the rest, and dark Buddy Holly glasses obscuring whatever thought may be going before him.

Me: "Isn't it hot?"

Orbison: "

Me: "Don't you think?"

Orbison: "

Marfa's Texas countryside is only rivaled by a few other areas I've visited: the outskirts of Hillsborough, some portions of New Mexico, and, above all, the hills of my hometown of Paso Robles on California's Central Coast.

On the way back to the motel, a storm passed just to the east, leaving behind a blue-black stillness in which two red-tailed hawks and one mangy buzzard never moved as we raced past them. They never looked above. I continued driving as if I were home. I looked to the hills to see if I could see my home in California, but it was not there. A sense of calm rushed over me, and I knew I'd make it through the film. It's a great sensation. I know the character dies, but what matters is that I will survive. I am getting better at living now. I've come to prefer it.

1984

The Goonies

NOVEMBER

The wind is blowing fiercely tonight, causing the boats in the harbor to collide. A pitch of light from someplace in the sky softly reflects off the sea. The melancholy ringing of bells through the town and port sounds off, as if they are emanating from inside a Hermann Hesse novel, weirdly ululating—and a fog-like nature towers over this calm, little, alcoholic community. I hear two men struggling to tie down their boat in frantic fits. I adore being here. Is this what it means to be in movies: a temporary existence, a taste of something that will not last?

2006

No Country

JULY

Joel arrived at Mary's evening feeling a little buzzed. He was telling stories about him and Ethan in the early days, like how they were mugged and one of the muggers sat on Ethan's chest and wouldn't let him get up; how they drove door to door in Minnesota with a teaser print of Blood Simple, trying to get money from the neighbors to finish it; and how Fran refuses to do press.

I like listening to him without any filters. He was watching a good short film that went on for far too long. Things are becoming looser here.

1984

The Goonies

NOVEMBER

Today is my day off. I miss my parents for some reason. It's night, and I'm watching boats pass by softly. I can hear the faint echo of a bird's cackle. My room smells like a sewer. Robert Davi terrifies me. He believes he is a genuine Fratelli. He glances at me with maniacal eyes, as if he's killed tiny punk kids before. Perhaps this is what acting entails: believing you are the person you are playing. Does that imply that to be decent, I must always wear these blue shorts over my gray sweatpants?

We're heading back to Los Angeles soon to work on a stage. Instead of filming in the actual sea, they will reconstruct the interiors of what remains to be shot to make filming easier. I understand that. They won't let us view the large boat until immediately before we shoot. I want to see it immediately, but Steven doesn't want us to—just because Steven doesn't want us to.

2006

No Country

JULY

Room 115. 11:45 a.m. I just woke up and went outside to take in my view of the parking lot. As I move under the gray cloud cover, a tickle of rain falls, and the motel door opens behind me. Then came a heavy downpour of hail and hard water. The parking lot is completely flooded, and the streets are all heavy torrents flowing in the same way.

I remember my mother holding that .22 rifle on her lover because she did not want him to leave. I recall the turmoil of my two children's births, and the first moment of potential life when their mother and I waited for them to breathe their first breath. I remember traveling alone up Interstate 5 and seeing random coyote fur entangled in barbed wire, and tractor-crossing signs peppered with gunshot holes spread throughout the West. I recall saying no when I discovered the girl was a virgin, went outside, sitting in a plastic chair, and tilting my head back while the rain dropped hard on my face.

I stand here under this stream of water falling from the sky, and the entire world stops to watch it unfold.

1985

The Goonies

JANUARY

They led us backwards. We were instructed to place our hands over our eyes. Several folks assisted us in navigating so that we wouldn't trip while going down the ramp. "Don't look!" Donner continued shrieking, and gradually our shoes, shins, thighs, and waists were submerged, totally clothed. "Still not looking!He laughed. Others were laughing.

They set up the first shot so we would react naturally. The aim was to completely immerse us, then use an underwater speaker to cue us when to pop up, turn around, and expose One-Eyed Willy's pirate ship, which they'd spent the previous year building within Warner Bros.' largest and deepest stage.

They lined us up. "Underwater!" We all took a deep breath and dived under. I opened my eyes to see a fuzzy speaker and rays of light piercing through the surface and onto the pool-like bottom. This was incredibly bizarre. We had been longing to see this thing for months. It all boiled down to this moment; whether or not it appeared in the film was irrelevant—it was the buildup, the experience that mattered. The ship appears near the end of the film, and when it eventually bursts free from the cave, we'll be finished and go our separate ways.

"And so on. ..NOW!!!" The muffled voice travelled underwater. I looked beside me to check whether it was time, but all I saw were legs. I rushed and turned, trying not to be too late and ruin the entire scene. I spotted a ship. It was farther away than I had expected. The interior of the stage was larger than I expected. But there it was: a giant pirate ship in an even larger body of water, submerging the entire stage. The mast and crow's nest on top almost reached the sky, and gold shone through the windows of the captain's quarters.

"Holy Shit!" I yelled. FUCK!" I was not acting. I said this. "FUCK!" Organic. I'd never seen anything like it. It was bigger than life, more than my teenage imagination could handle.

"CUT! Fuck???"

"Sorry."

"You cannot say fuck in this film!"

"I understand. "I am sorry."

The kids all laughed, and I laughed as well, although knowing I had made a mistake. It was a fucking pirate ship created on a stage in a movie studio in the valley of Los Angeles. I do not know, guy. They should have warned me.

2006

No Country

AUGUST

Luce Rains. That is his name. That is his stage name. I'm not sure what his real name is. He received a shot to the throat tonight. He was shot first in the throat, then the head. He had a lot to say beforehand, and we all found out that he manages the Shakespeare Festival in Santa Fe.

JOEL: Okay, I'm going to count three, two, one as you raise your head.

LUCE: Three, two, or one?

JOEL: Yes. Three, two, one as you lift your head.

LUCE: But wait. Wait. How about a bang? I need a bang.

JOEL: Then we'll say "Bang." We're going to make an impact.

LUCE: Good. I need that bang. (Then to me.) What if I just pass you a joint? ..?ME: What?

LUCE: I feel like I should simply pass you a joint, smoke it, and then pass it over. (I look at Andy, the focus puller, and he turns his head away.)

BETSY (assistant director): OK, REHEARSAL!

LUCE: (starts maniacally clearing his throat) Hrururuummmmm. ..Getting punchy.

ME: Dude, relax. Just relax.

Joel: And. ..We're ready. ..TAKE ACTION. ..Three times. ..two . ..one . ...wait! No. Your head.

LUCE: Okay. Okay. Okay, fair enough. How about three, two, one gargle gargle gargle? Then back?

Ethan starts giggling and turns his head away. Roger Deakins is staring at his small wheel monitor with the expression of someone who has just taken a large amount of lithium.

JOEL: Just three, two, one, and you'll feel the air rush out of your brain. You will not have to worry about it.

LUCE: I GET IT! Yes. Oh. Gargle, three, two, and one—Bang! Are you going to say "Bang!"?"?

JOEL: You do not need to worry about it. You will feel the air.

LUCE: Is it a comedy? (Luce begins to chuckle uncontrollably while everyone else looks at their feet.)

Roger moves slightly in his seat.

BETSY: ANOTHER REHEARSAL! READY!

LUCE: (to me) These people are great.

ME: Yes. For their first film.

LUCE: No way, man! They've done like—

BETSY: READY?

LUCE: fuck. Gargle. Gargle. Three, two, and one.

Joel: And. ..We're ready. ..Take action. ..Three times. ..two . ..What are you doing?!

LUCE: (Gargle gargle gargle). ..sorry?

JOEL: You can't lift your head that much. We cannot see you. We need to see the hit.

LUCE: So three, two, one, hit, bang, and back.

Bruce, the dolly grip, is holding on to the crane and has tears in his eyes from laughing so hard. The right side of Keith's (Props) mustache twitches.

LUCE: (to me) I've heard about your collarbone. What happened?

ME: What?

LUCE: your collarbone. Do you ride?

ME: . ..um. Yeah.

LUCE: Me, too. Gargle. Gargle. Hack!

BETSY: READY!

ETHAN: Let us shoot!

JOEL: Let us shoot!

BETSY: ROLLING!

LUCE: I'd like to pass the joint. ..ME: . ..dude.

LUCE: gargle. Gargle. Gargle. How did you get this role?

JOEL: I'm ready. ..and . ..ACTION! Three! Two! One!

The air compressor failed, and Luce Rains' neck exploded. Everyone behind the monitor chuckled as I was stunned and scared. He'd distracted me with the question, "How did you get this role?"

For the rest of the night, Peter (Special Effects) sprayed blood in my face with a metal pipe. And there was Luce Rains among the crew: prosthetics hanging from his neck and head, tubes protruding from either side, looking around, making constant thumbs-up gestures in my direction, and egging me on between takes about how we should do a production of Othello together once I finished this little film.

1985

The Goonies

MARCH

We're in Bodega Bay, California, shooting the film's ending. My mother is here. I needed to bring her. It would have been too humiliating not to, given that I was with my father's friend for the majority of the shoot. She is my mother, and I would be a bad son not to include her.

I warned her on the plane that she had to maintain a low profile, which she disliked: "What am I meant to do, nothing?" Everything is always at the extreme. My ex-girlfriend abandoned Santa Barbara and our misfit collective, the Cito Rats. She lives up here now—my high school sweetheart—so I'll probably spend the majority of my free time with her. Staci was gold when I first met her at Santa Barbara High. She had a radiance about her that resembled the pristine West Coast beaches we played on as children. She had a purity, which became infected shortly after she began seeing me. The Cito Rats were a misfit community that depended on themselves. My attraction to her was not the same as her attraction to me. She needed to spice things up. I needed a way out. She won.

After just a few days of shooting, my mother called me in the middle of the night. She had gone out with several of the show's crew members. When she returned to her hotel room, she heard a knock on the door. It was one of the producers. He asked to enter. She allowed him. He dropped his pants and wanted to get to them. She's telling me this, and then she says, "If you think I'd fuck someone who wears blue boxer shorts, you gotta be outta your mind." This is my mother. Our producer. This movie. It's impossible to have her here and not have anything like this happen. She brings it with her.

Today, the producer called me into his office and informed me that my mother is sick and may require assistance. I listened as he told me more about her and expressed his concern for me. After he paused to let it all sink in like a terrible actor in a bad movie, I asked, "Because she wouldn't fuck you?" He asked me to leave his office when he began to shake.

Given that I have a little of my mother in me, I believe we have no place in the film industry. It's a nice bunch, and while the circus frenzy is appealing, it's nothing like the Cito Rats. At least it is. We'll see if people enjoy this film, or if they think I'm any good. It doesn't really matter. If this isn't it, I'll find something else. Like my mother, I am resourceful.

2006

No Country

AUGUST

This was Javier's last day. They prepared a cake for him with miniature two-by-three-inch photographs of everyone he'd murdered in the film on it. That, and everyone donned hairnets on his last day, just like he did to keep his hair in place during shooting. The show has nearly ended. On stage, it feels like a damp coat. We're on stage, and the light blinds when you go outside. I sense a headache coming on.

Tommy Lee entered the makeup trailer this morning. I will miss him, although we never worked together.

"Are you aware that Llewellyn Moss is from San Saba County?"

"I did know that."

"It's been the same for a hundred and fifty years."

"I'm sure."

"It's not a stupid place."

"I understand."

I peeked out the trailer window and saw Joel and Ethan preparing a shot. They resembled Laurel and Hardy, except both, not one, were horribly skinny.

I wish my mom was on set. I miss the sense that anything may happen at any time, outside of me.

Last week, a crew member handed out shirts that read I BLAME JOSH BROLIN and featured a photo of my intoxicated face from one of those weekends of debauchery, complete with a cowboy hat and a huge, idiot smile.

I'm going to miss being here.

The desert.

Everything exudes a Dr. Seussian vibe.

The monsoons.

The brothers.

It's ridiculous, this storytelling business. We are children playing in a sandbox filled with our own toys. I prefer it, I've realized, if only for the company of people who are sincerely attempting to exorcise the spinning visions in their thoughts.

1985

The Goonies

JANUARY

I just read a letter from my mother.

Josh, I am really proud of you! You've had a lot of experience in the last several years. Growing up is extremely difficult, and you made it even more difficult than it already was. But you've come out of it as a perfectly responsible, put-together individual. This tells me you genuinely enjoy it all. Please work harder in school since you will always be able to apply your knowledge. We are continually learning, every day. Allow yourself to be good to yourself and those around you. I adore and admire you greatly. Thanks for bringing me here. I had a lot of fun—I love you very much, Mom.

I have to return to school now. I heard they're doing Guys and Dolls. I believe I might audition for one of the minor roles. I'll head back up to see my friends. I haven't been drinking in a while. The last time I tried to start that fire, I had no idea the gas had been on for so long. It still signs my brows.

I will also drink with my mother. Her appearance on the film felt like a fix after she kicked me out of the house. I went to live on my father's couch. He was residing with the girl in her apartment.

I'm delighted she's proud of me for doing that movie. I have made life more difficult than it needed to be. I am aware of this. We all do. I miss my friends. I just want to return to what was. I am a Cito Rat. I shall always be.

CHAPTER 3
THROUGH THE GLASS, DARKLY

*O*NCE UPON A TIME, there was a mother, a father, a child, and a large number of animals. They were a family, and they lived in a house with lights, a kitchen for cooking, and carpet that resembled the fur of a shaggy brown dog. They dwelt in that house under a sun and a moon that came and went with the seasons, and the days were long, as were the nights, especially. When the nights came, the moon shone, the dogs barked, the cats meowed, the father left, the mother yelled, and Little Johnny simply existed.

One night, the mother called the phone several times in an attempt to locate the father, who was out driving, walking, playing with his buddies, or hiding, and she was yelling into that dark and heavy phone that never responded. Little Johnny was four years old at the time, and he was an only child, as his brother, Jess (who was supposed to be a girl), would not be born until the following winter. But it was summer now—a sultry, damp night in the San Fernando Valley—and the moon was high in the sky, peering through the clouds and shining brightly on Little Johnny's face. The mother shouted into the phone behind him about assholes, another lady, and hell, and threatened to set fire to the house if he didn't return home. Little Johnny had heard the yelling before, but he didn't comprehend the words very well. He enjoyed the flames, but not inside the house. He had a sudden thought to feed the mother of the little mice in the small plastic container in his room, the pink ones who squeaked, squealed, and writhed. He remembered those babies and how they sucked at their mother's teats. He pictured himself sucking at a mother's teats, feeling as if he were floating in a thick cloud with no rain and never-ending warmth. He liked listening to those newborn mice because they sounded like helium laughter, which made him chuckle as if he were a member of their family. But for the time being, he glanced up at the moon in the sky, and the moon returned his gaze. He exhaled, and the breath fogged the window before him.

The mother behind him shouted and hurled the phone down, shattering the glass table beneath it. He was shocked, and he glanced at the moon again, trying not to shake. The mother dashed across the hallway to the back of the house, past his bedroom to where hers was, and lay face down on the hard bed with the thin floral cover. There was no moon on that side of the house, so Little Johnny waved goodbye to it and followed his mother along the corridor, despite his fear. When he reached the end of the bed, where the mother's toes pointed to the floor, he touched her ankle, causing her to weep. The mother rarely cried. She enjoyed yelling much more.

After a long time, my father returned home. The lights were turned off inside the house, and Johnny was petting the mother's head with his small hand. A red tint flooded over the hallway walls, and the engine of the father's truck fell silent. The mother stood up and dashed into the silence, leaving Little Johnny to hear only the soft weight of her footsteps. Little Johnny could see the dark blue in the sky above the odd-shaped pool where his father liked to swim back and forth while holding his breath, indicating that daylight was approaching. Little Johnny would sometimes grab his father's shoulders while he swam underwater and try to hold his breath as long as the father did. He aspired to be like his father, who was tall, quiet, and gorgeous, and whom most people admired.

The coffee mugs that the mother had purchased in Mexico the previous summer were just missing the father's head as he walked down the brick walkway of the family's home. The glass windows through which Little Johnny looked at the moon and the moon looked back at him were no longer there. The windows were now in sharp bits all over the carpet, which resembled curly brown dog hair, and the grass, which had just been mowed the day before. The mother yelled and told the father to go, despite the fact that he had just arrived. The mother was upset since the father had left and was now present at the family's house. Little Johnny observed and reflected on how he learnt about numbers in school. He knew that when you have one and one, it equals two. But there was one of the mother, one of the father, and one of himself, and he had no idea what that meant. And there were a lot of numbers on the ground now, and he felt horrible for them; all those numbers on the ground didn't add up to anything, Little Johnny reasoned. He enjoyed the window when it was open, and he liked the moon when it was too. And he thought of himself as one, and he liked it that way.

The father got back in his truck, the red lights turned back on, and they slowly drove away down the driveway. The dogs barked. The mother wiped her nose and opened the cupboards to prepare pancakes. Little Johnny fed the mother of the mice in the plastic container in his room and checked off his blue duty chart on the wall, hoping that once all of the chore boxes were checked, he'd get the bag with six pockets he'd been wanting.

The phone rang when Little Johnny was eating his pancakes. The mother reached across the broken numbers on the floor to pick it up. There was conversation, smiles, laughter. Little Johnny imagined piñatas, rainbows, and The Cat in the Hat pictures. As the sun rose, dogs stopped barking and lay down in the mud, resting their long chins on crossed-over paws. And through the broken windows, Little Johnny saw the moon in the distance as she walked gently down the driveway, departing softly as the red lights had just moments ago.

1990

The prison where Gary Gilmore was executed sparkles as we pass by. Prisons have always triggered some strange fishtailing activity in the back of my mind. They are alive. Maybe it wants to be recognized in me: concealed conditions that have suddenly burst through the guardrails of my denial and careened over the bridge into the seething cauldron of my own terrible mistakes?

Snow covers everything.

The significant differences in climate across states make me anxious, as if the strange area on the other side of a boundary is a barrier we weren't supposed to traverse. The hills get more solid as one travels further into Wyoming. Greys and reds. Mars Dust. Eroded, but strong. The hillslopes are carved with dramatic geometric shadows and lights that greet us as we pass through them. Again, it makes me anxious, as if I'm playing a game bigger than myself, one over which I have no control.

The stink of the next sorry town draws me in like a magnet: garbage-filled creeks, fast food, and plastic microwavable dinners. There is no culture, nor is there any hope of finding something coherent. A petri dish of self-destruction. We park and stroll across a bleak lot that appears to have seen dozens of deaths. The doors scream as we enter and moan through corrosion as they open. Inside, my youngster bounces through the aisles as an innocent should.

Later, his mother was ticketed for speeding in Rawlins, Wyoming: 75 mph in a 65. We spent two hours in Rawlins drafting comments to the sheriff's office explaining why she was right to speed and the charges were incorrect. These attempts rarely work, except for my mother's twenty-page run-on diatribes. She was always able to get out of the ninety-five in twenty-five speeding tickets. Us? Never.

Once we're back on the road, the sun begins to set, transforming the sky into velvet in deep reds and yellow-oranges. Thick clouds lean against the sun in bright hellish colors: vermillion, furious, and blood reds. I almost caused an accident by gazing behind me, but the colors are giving me something I wish I could recover later, but I won't be able to. Its beauty gives me the same jolt as watching my son sleep, but it only lasts as long as it does. It's short-lived because things are only alive for as long as I believe they are, and I don't always have the right to do so. So it dies, short-lived and beyond my control.

The sun departs, and I return my attention to the road. Nobody is speaking. The windows are slightly open, and a small whirlwind of wind swirls around the interior of the vehicle. My nose appears broken in the rearview mirror. Low clouds running parallel to us increase. We're going rapidly. Three people. A youthful family. Faster than we can.

2004

(Cocoon)

I'm going to drink wine from a glass from now on. I'll get the glass from a flea market; it should be rough to the touch and pink or blue, like old, cheap church windows. I'll hold it at its base and press my fingernail against its rim, listening for its value, but there will be none hanging in the air, so I'll smile. It will be a glass similar to those on the dish rack at Old Man Wiebe's house, next to the crumbling Formica table and just above the worn sallow linoleum floor. It will have been touched by those who work hard and sweat every day, and those who wait for their spouses to return home. It will have been used by those who had just completed the dishes and noticed their fat men across the room, in lazy recliners, peering back over their shoulders with sexy eyes and phantom sounds of four-poster pine mattresses creaking violently. It will be a muddy glass, with a man's hand just off the tractor after plowing hundreds of acres of oats, his lungs spinning with dust. This glass will be valuable solely because it is completely American: accessible and tasteless. I'll sip from this glass grocery store wine, enduring headaches long before I fall asleep.

I'll fill my glass and then raise it to those who have touched it before, the rough hands of gentle people who bloom and wilt like flowers.

1988

"I'm having a baby," I informed him. He merely stood there, staring at me, one eye squinting as if it were being partially blinded by the sunlight. "Did you hear me? I'm having a baby. Not you," he finally responded. "What do you mean? Not me. "Yes, me."

I hadn't been to jail yet. I'd been a couple times, but not recently.

"When?"

"Summer."

"You're nineteen."

"Yep."

"Are you going to have a baby this summer?"

"That's right."

I thought to myself, "Why not?" I wanted to have children for as long as I can remember. Sure, I drank excessively. My mother did too, and I did it well.

"You might want to rethink it."

"Fuck you, dude. I'm having a child. It's going to be fantastic."

To support my belief that I'd always wanted to have children, I'd been carrying around a small school photo of a friend's little girl for months. In a trailer at work, I showed someone the photo and informed her that it was my one-and-a-half-year-old.

"Aw, she's so cute."

Thank you. And she wrote on the reverse, 'I love you, Daddy.'"

"How old is she?"

"Year and a half. "Eighteen months."

"So she wrote that?"

"Yeah. Isn't it sweet?"

"She didn't write that."

"Yes, she did. 'Daddy, I adore you.' See?"

"Kids that age can't write."

"Well, she can."

"No, she can't."

"It's right there."

Her tenacity made me panicky. She discovered something about me. I am a fraud.

"No, not you" wasn't going to work. It's gotta be me. I'm going to be fine as a parent, am I? I'm going to teach my children how to accomplish things. I'm going to be the powerful example I've always wanted to be.

I had served a jail sentence for assaulting cops, then spent months in a halfway house in Pasadena with fifteen other guys, riding my Harley through a deep frost to our flat on Franklin Avenue in the heart of Hollywood to attend Bradley Method childbirth classes someplace in the Valley:

Breathe once. ..two . ..Three times. ..four. Breathe once. ..two . ..Three times. ..four. Now push!

I am capable of doing this. We've got an apartment. I'm sober now. After this, I'll have to pedal my bike back to Pasadena and the halfway house. Flannel shirts. Leather jacket. No helmet. It's cold. Train yourself to envision the heat in Hawaii, Africa, or somewhere other than here. I am hot. It is not working. I'm starting to burn up. No, I am freezing to death. Get there. Park and lock the bike. Thaw your hands. Now for the nightly group meeting with all the guys. Ron, the man who runs the residence, is short and stocky. His black fingers are chalky, and the ends of them have calluses, but I'm not sure why, other than when he knocks them against the top of the table that separates us.

"The hairon took me down," he says. I had nothing left. I would have sucked your dick if you had asked me, but all I could think about was the hair. It was like water to a man in the desert with nothing but a bag of potato chips. Do you hear me?"

Go upstairs. Get on your knees and lay your elbows on the small twin mattress with the thin, smoky cover that a hundred other desperate men have used before me.

Dear God.

Help me realize that this is the start of a journey I can be proud of. I am twenty years old, and I am open to whatever course you deem fit. Thank you for the chance. (I can't be a decent father.) Thank you for the change. (I cannot do this.) Amen.

When she was finally ready to give birth months later, she went through forty-four hours of progressive labor. When he appeared, he was dark blue. It wasn't like in the movies, where the infant was pink and the size of a nine-month-old. He was small, defenseless, and limping. The doctor positioned him face down on his forearm and began to pat his back with his meaty palm. We were advised that the throat could become lodged. Mucus. Get it loose. He only needed his first breath. Meat hand tapped slightly harder. The nurses looked on. What's happening? said his mother. What is happening? I do not know. He isn't a living color. He isn't moving. Why doesn't he move?! This marks the beginning for us. This is the remainder of our life, right now, in this room, this hospital. Everything changes here.

To establish what is actually going on, you look at people's eyes. You can't concentrate on their looks. They tell lies. The face can change shape, but the eyes cannot lie for long, especially if the person cares. So I observed my son while I contemplated losing him before he was even born. How? Who should I blame for this? Then I looked at the doctor's eyes.

They changed. He looked at a nurse, who ran out the door. You changed. Something is very wrong. Everyone has changed. There is panic. This is no longer a question.

"I'm having a baby," I informed him. He merely stood there, staring at me, one eye squinting as if it were being partially blinded by the sunlight. "Did you hear me? I'm having a baby. Not you," he finally responded. "What do you mean? Not me. "Yes, me."

The next day, the nurses entered our room. Debby was on the bed, recovering, and I was in the recliner with Trevor next to me. We were all exhausted, but sleeping with a newborn next to you, I've discovered, isn't sleeping. It's time to rest your eyes.

We were given birth certificate documents. I filled it out. Our son had survived. He came through. He didn't want to let go of the mucus that was caught in his throat.

The nurses checked Trevor, smiled and left the paperwork. I thought, "Wow, we just named our child." He will go by that name for the rest of his life.

Debby called the nurses just then. The door opened and she asked to see paperwork. There was a pause before she looked up, partly smiling and half angry off. "Are you serious?"

"What?"

"You left the s out."

"Of what?"

"His name. It reads: Trevor Manur Brolin. "Like manure."

"What? "No, I did not."

"Look."

And there it was: Trevor Manur Brolin. The nurses were giggling. Debby switched it back to Mansur.

I gazed at Trevor in the chair. Pink. He was now a deep pink: still little, defenseless, and healthy. The music started when the baby drew his first breath. I can't explain it, but it's music that will always be ascribed to him.

I am having a baby.

Yes, it's me.

CHAPTER 4
A LAND OF MISFITS

*D*uring a table buffet breakfast in Austin, Texas, a famous writer recommended that I read a new novel called No Country for Old Men. He is no longer alive, however he remains well-known. I was in the middle of telling him about a dinner I once had with a legendary actor who fell asleep during a conversation over wine while we, the group, asked him about streetcars and waterfronts and the like, as well as other encounters with other famous famous types who he didn't consider particularly famous because, I'm sure, his fame far outweighed theirs. He only mentioned one woman with long nose hairs, a very renowned woman whose name he couldn't recall because his popularity dwarfed hers. We understood who he was referring to, but she was only a distant memory for him.

The famous writer looked at me as if he wasn't interested (which piqued my interest in impressing him), so I told him another story about another legendary actor who attempted to seize my mother's ranch shortly after she died, and that actor is still alive and famous, but one of the few whose shows haven't been canceled, which is extremely interesting given his age and arrogance, which would have buried most people today.

But the famous infamous writer was still not impressed, and I thought to myself, what could possibly be the problem other than that I, the storyteller at this point, might not be famous enough to elicit the default-worthy, mouth-to-the-sky guffaw that morphs into what might be interpreted as. ..Well, enthusiasm and, of course, interest.

I mentioned many encounters with the greats, the very thing I know most famous people are interested in hearing: comparable stories about other famous people doing ordinary things that are discovered and incorporated into mythology, and stories that keep said famous people intriguing and unique. I told him about an actor almost unknown at the time and me walking the streets of Vancouver during the days of 21 Jump Street, drunk, hair combed back, scrolling for girls into the late last hours of the pleasant all-too-nicely-Canadian night; and, also, about the time I was celebrating with beers with a method-y-type actor with a prominent nose and a famous upper lip in a too-bright Palmdale motel lobby after my last day on Inherent Vice (he later, incidentally There was also the time I danced with one of my favorite actors in a Toronto bar and squeezed his buns and he yelled at me and I smiled and was happy because everyone heard him yell at me and that's what I wanted anyway, and there was that time I insulted another actor-turned-director's sweater at the Chateau Marmont, apologizing to his agent the next day (because that's what famous people do: apologize to famous people's famous agents or assistants, not the famous people themselves). Said agent revealed to me that I had been blacked-out rude to the famous actor in the bad sweater, to which I replied that being rude is part of the game, but that now is the time for a Step 9 amends, and could he please give me the famous-person-who-I-insulted phone number so I could do this properly, to which he replied that I should know better than to ask for any famous person's personal phone number.

There was New Orleans, that time, when I ran, naked, after a younger, more aspiring actress, into the French Quarter, and hit my head so hard tripping after her that it split the flesh down to the skull while she yelled at me to get my ass back inside, but I don't remember that time so well, but, damn, do I love New Orleans and the love affair I had with her: the way that town fucked me and the way I fucked it back is etched haphazardly into an elusive memory as I was at

And I recall a day in London (it occurred so quickly) when another little, but older, actress whispered in my ear, "Twenty years ago I would have fucked you silly." That occurred.

But the writer has yet to respond, not even with a yawn.

I am breaking down as I stare at him. We sit in silence, and as we do so, images of other people come to me that I can't think would impress him. They impressed me. That is what I am left with. I am remembering. I'm attempting to recall guys and women who briefly entered my mind after introducing themselves before being released like unwanted balloons. But these faces are somehow imprinted on me because of what they said to me or how they changed my life with that odd, inadvertent gift of theirs. What about the young girl I met at Copenhagen's rail station when I was eighteen? Isn't this essential to you? The one I took to get hot fries and who sobbed as I departed for my train four hours later. We fell in love for a few hours, and the image of her lying on her side on the concrete in that train station always brings back warm memories and serves as a reminder that not every transaction is permanent. And what about that hooker in Paris, whose golden hair I can still feel tenderly against my hand? How I attempted to persuade her to come travel with me despite bad translations. How I pictured us living a life on the road, me writing and her as a seamstress or working with children. Or what about the chap in Ireland who brought me golfing near the Cliffs of Moher? How patient he was with me. What a beautiful day to be humbled. Or on that journey through Cuba with the kids and the elderly woman who invited us into her dirt-floor home and poured the rest of her coffee? The kids looked to me for approval, and I said, "We're going to get sick because of the water," but we all knew it was the gracious thing to do, to accept it and drink it with her since we'd remember her generosity for the rest of our lives. Or the woman in Scotland, on the Isle of Skye, who gave us the trailer in her backyard for the night if the B&B down the street didn't have any beds at this late hour: "Anything for these two little sweeties." My home will become your home. Just come back if things don't work out."

There is no great writer I am referring to anymore; it is simply everyone's story as they fight and dance in their own suffering.

1987

I'm really starting to feel like I don't have a mother. I want to call her, but I can't bring myself to do it.

I keep getting out of bed in the middle of the night and wind up on the couch. It's from so many years of couch surfing that it's become a habit.

I intend to relocate to New York after this series, Private Eye, is completed. I truly do not want to travel to Santa Barbara anymore. The Cito Rats scene is still thriving. People are beginning to die. Every time I go up there, I end up in jail, in a car accident, or in a fight. I have no friends here. I'm alone, except when I'm drinking. I'll fuck any lady and then give them some fake phrase as if I'm trying to save a non-existent relationship. Why? Are the people I meet as crazy as I am, or is it all a ruse to turn on each other when we least expect it?

My mother does not want to see me. My father cares but is caught up in the jet stream of his own celluloid-created universe.

This adolescent brain is a hamster wheel of never-ending, pointless thoughts.

Perhaps I should just pick up and call her.

February 12, 1995.

Tonight I got a call from my brother. It was late, and I did not want to pick up. I'm in New York. The New York where smoke still covers the streets and depravity screams loudly down alleyways before entering a larger arena of dirty air. I feed off the electricity here, the people: there is grit and character everywhere, and now, out of sleep, my cells are reacting to the subtle friction of a voice I haven't heard in a long time.

"Mom got into a really bad accident."

"Yeah, what's new?"

"No, I think this one"—his voice drops—"is really bad."

My brother never calls me. Never. He does not especially like me. It must be awful enough for him to phone me, yet he doesn't seem distraught. Something is off here.

"Where is she?"

"I do not know. The hospital, I suppose. "It was a car wreck."

"She's always involved in car accidents. Why is this one different?"

"I don't know."

There's a long pause. He does not know what to say. I am exhausted. I understand this is different. I need to get up. I turn on the floor lamp, but the light hurts my eyes. I know my life is about to change. I got a feeling in my chest.

"All right. How do you know? Where is she?"

"Dad called me. I do not know."

"Okay."

"See ya."

I'm wearing my underwear. Bare feet. I step out into the living room, illuminated by the streetlamps outside. I can see some of the Soldiers' and Sailors' Monument on Eighty-Ninth Street. I sat on the windowsill with my son. The elderly lady across the street would always call the fire department whenever we sat up there. My son adored firefighters, so this was ideal for him. He was never in danger since the windowsill was broad and constructed of concrete, and I always had my arm wrapped around him. We would sit there eagerly waiting for the approaching sirens.

One night, a lone man dressed in full Scottish garb, kilt and everything, was playing his bagpipes. When we went up to sit on the windowsill, the fog was so thick that we couldn't see him.

I can hear the pipes like they're playing right now. I can feel my son's hand inside mine. I don't want to phone my father, but I realize I have to. Moving forward into this new dimension of my existence necessitates movement. I do not want to move. My mother has died. I know it. I can feel it moving within me. Something is different.

"Hello?"

"Pop?"

"Hey."

"Where is she?"

"Paso. "Twin cities."

"How are you doing?"

"She's still alive, but nothing's happening. "She's not there."

She is not there. What does this mean? She was chasing her lover in her large Suburban at the time. I know this person. I attended school with him. He was slightly older than I was. He was tall and lithe, with many freckles. I never got it: she was 55, he was 30. It must have been good to be appealing to a younger man. However, he harbored resentment toward her. She was a tough woman who handed it out frequently. She would ride them till they wanted to get out of the automobile. Take Joyce, for example. Joyce was a friend of hers, and between driving at over 100 mph and my mother's continual bombardment of hillbilly rhetoric, she once wanted to get out of the car. She wanted out although she could only see dust and rattlesnakes for fifty miles. So my mother slammed on the breaks, let her out, and drove away. She did not pretend to drive away and then return to make up. That was not her style. She departed and probably never thought of returning. I'm sure Joyce caught a lift from the next trucker passing by, because they were best friends again within a week. That's how it was with my mother.

However, slenderness with freckles was an angry tool. Not country or eighteen-wheeler angry, but tractor angry, poke-the-animal angry, and unable to speak back to father angry.

"You have horrible tits. "Ugly tits."

"You are a piece of garbage; I had cancer. I had an infection!"

"You are old, though. Why am I even with you? What the fuck am I doing here? "I am leaving."

"No, you're not."

"Fuck you! I'm leaving here."

They drank that night. They'd traveled to Cambria, and she adored the dive bar there. It was a long way away, but it was different from AJ Spurs, which she visited far too frequently anyhow.

"Fuck you, Jane." Take your lousy house and ranch, and go fuck yourself.

She pulled a .22 caliber firearm on him.

"You're not going anywhere."

"Are you kidding me?!"

Guns are a part of everyday life where we come from. Danny shot himself on the street when he was fourteen. His heart was empty. Shit happens in the country, but no one ever blames guns.

So, while the gun appeared to be a threat, it was actually not. ..Until it was.

"Sit down."

"Fuck you!" . ..He stepped out the door. She probably considered firing a bullet into him. I am sure she thought about it.

She had cancer years ago. They had removed one breast, and then the silicone implant had become infected. They needed to remove it before it contaminated the rest of her body, so she was left with a flap for a bit, at least until they reinflated the dead titty. The guilt must have been too much, along with the age gap and the romance on the decline from previous days, when she informed me with childlike playfulness that he didn't enjoy it when she tried to insert her finger into his buttocks.

He followed him along the dusty road in his rickety old truck, while she drove her bloated green Suburban. He was far ahead, and she could not see him. Just past the ranch where I grew up, after the long straight through the hanging witch's hair and the one lit sign that my father had helped carve years earlier, was a bend that turned down and to the left.

There was little trace of braking. There was just approximately a foot-long skid mark on the dirt before the tree. I'm sure she was reaching for something and was pushed down further than she thought because she was already turning left. A typical Jane speed of about seventy in a thirty-five was not uncommon. She hit the tree, and it wasn't moving.

Old Man Barlogio heard it from his home. It was around 9:30 a.m. when he climbed into his pickup and drove out to the end of his driveway to Vineyard, the main road. The Suburban's front was smashed. He got to her. His strong rancher fingers raised her head. She was scarcely breathing, but she was breathing nonetheless. Nobody expected Jane to die, least of all us. She was protected by a character so distinct and distinctive that death would be an insult to her legend. She'd be leaving behind a gentle wind, a clear sky, and no music on the radio. She was the zap in every electrical current we had experienced. She was the alcohol in a mixed cocktail. She was the wildness in a sunset right after a terrible storm passed.

But there was blood everywhere, so he tenderly lowered her head, walked back across the street, unlocked his truck door with a metal pop, and drove back down his dirt lane to the front of his house. The black rotary dial phone sat just past the kitchen as you entered the living room on the left, on a little side table next to his one camel-colored EZ chair. He snatched it up and dialed nine, one, and then another.

She died just after midnight. I instructed them to pull the plug. There was nothing left. I spoke with a family friend, a radiologist we knew, on the phone before I boarded the plane:

"What is the reality?"

"Son, she's gone. She's being kept alive entirely by machines."

"Where's the miracle in this? Is there one?"

"No. This is for you now. "Not for her."

"Okay."

Then dial a tone.

2018

I am watching pink and blue candy cotton clouds form below. I'm traveling north through marine layers and various weather systems. I've had dreams about bouncing on clouds (I was naked in the dream) and then plunging through them, with condensation and electrical static tickling my body. Would I pass someone just getting off the Golden Gate Bridge? Would we be able to fall together for a second and exchange one last conscious look? Would we scare the life back into ourselves? Death is a weird dream, and dreams are usually the most intriguing pastime. I can't fit through the plane's little oval window, though. I have gained too much weight. Will I fall differently if I'm in better shape? Now there is snow. We've gotten over mountains. I can feel the cold, and I see ice building on my plan. It's too cold to jump now. I will wait. I will order a coffee. The flight attendant who wanted to speak about movies will now give me an attitude since all I wanted to do was look out the window—peace at thirty thousand feet. How many minutes would I fall? There's something about a winged animal falling through the air that conjures a more lovely image than a pig in a pen, an elephant with someone on his back, or a three-legged dog on Tijuana's streets asking for water, everyone avoiding him but later chatting about it.

2006

(A letter.)

Dearest, Wally

Okay, I declined the sinister opportunity to work with TLJ again with that director. Why? I'm not sure yet, but they're in New Mexico filming something, which is better than nothing, but the part offered was given to another actor, which confirmed my belief that the role was better suited to Marlon's quirky friend (let's call him Andy) than to Marlon himself. I noticed no motorcycles for the character, no jazz joints, no "pop" to drink, and certainly no "birds to dig on, Daddy O." That director just doesn't understand us, Wally. They don't realize we're from another era, right?

Instead, I am at home, having just returned from racing automobiles in the Salinas Valley. I placed third twice. I started in the back both times and worked my way to third. My only preparation for each race was watching "Play Misty for Me." Don't ask why; I'm not sure. I just know it worked like a charm.

I've completed writing the submarine movie (which I believe is fantastic), and I'm ready for you to see it. It's a little long right now (354 pages), but we can work on removing a few superfluous bits here and there if you think it's essential. It does not take place in Fargo anymore. The little town adjacent to it (Wahpeton) has the same accent. Same cast (as previously stated), but different time of year (the snow MUST melt—I can't move on that one), and I believe we should begin in the spring and conduct pickups in the. ..Blah blah blah, you understand. I'm completely open to recommendations, though. I've made a preliminary budget and will discuss it with you when I see you (it's a Russian sub, and I'm not sure how much we can obtain one for, but I've planned for it, and I believe they'll be reasonably priced).

Life isn't the same without you, Wally.

Continue to enjoy Hollywood Squares, and I'll continue to rev my bike until it finds itself close outside Belleview Medical Facility, where you'll be moseying down one of the few streets branching out from there, head down, coming up with a reason not to do my submarine movie because you're afraid that it will be so much better than that movie you did in the town next to the one mine takes place in (Yes, I'm calling mine "WAHPETON"—way better than "A SUBMARINE TALE BASED Anyway, read it. It's good.

Life isn't the same without you, Wally.

I went to Turks and Caicos, and the first night there, I seriously damaged my ankle. I gimped around that island with my "testicular problem," my graying beard, my atrophied shoulder, and my leg sticking out to one side in typical John Merrick style. I'm now known as "Boo Boo Brolin." It's unfortunate. I am a mess. That's why I'm racing again: I just want to end this.

Send me your mailing address.

Marlon

2021

(SANTA FE)

The cherry blossoms exploded overnight. Last night's sleep was disturbed by visions of witch hunts, mental frenzies, and some type of devilry. I awoke briefly but forced myself to return to sleep since the events were too exciting to miss. I should go outside this morning. I need to take something physical.

I go down the gravel before sitting down to look at images of my kid swimming in a pool while holding her breath. She glances into my eyes in the photo. She was barely several months old. Her expression is reminiscent of photos I've seen of Georgia O'Keeffe: a leathery smirk, brush in hand, evidence of months spent studying the holes in the dried bones of horses and steers, the colors she used for a mesa, the contours of a high desert hill as she stood there watching it all. Her expression conveys a strong sense of ownership. That's how it is. This is what I see in my daughter's eyes.

She holds her breath, suspended in a fresh and unexpected feeling, hoping that these experiences will open her up like the cherry blossoms above us, which are suddenly erupting with beauty and without warning.

CHAPTER 5
THROUGH THE DUST

*I*t's cold, and our sleeping bags are covered in a thin layer of shimmering frost. I can hear it crinkle as I bring the bag up to my chin. I have not opened my eyes yet. I also hear ducks running on the water's surface with the familiar titter-tat that I associate with growing up in the countryside. My father is next to me. We hunted yesterday. He handed me a 20-gauge shotgun and explained that we were going to shoot doves. I'm comfortable with a pistol. I've always been. I am consistent with violence, but it does not suit me. I vividly imagine the consequences: a grandmother squirrel crying for her favorite babe after it's been shot in the head; a terrified fox sobbing combing the ranch in an attempt to locate her now-dead progeny; a doe braying for her bambi. The thoughts plague me.

I shot two in one shot. The white doves lay lifeless, wrapped in a plastic bag and knotted off.

There is a low fog over the reservoir, which is under the rising sun. We made a tiny campfire and heated water, which my father then poured into a blue speckled tin cup. He pours instant coffee into it and stirs until all the grains have dissolved. When he places the cup in his lips, his lower lip twitches convulsively. It has always done that. I'm not sure why. I observe it as I press the fishing hook's point on the pad of my index finger.

The last time I went to this pond, I was with my entire family and a few friends. It was an extremely hot day. We were swimming as the adults drank beer and iced tea. There was the nineteen-year-old cowboy who seemed to be hanging about from down the road, the son of the old guy who would finally find my mother smashed against the oak tree across the street from his driveway. The cowboy son, I believe, had feelings for her.

The youngsters, including my younger brother, had spent the majority of the day playing in the muck algae at the pond's edge. I felt a sting on my foot. I yanked it out of the pond mud with a fart-y suction-y crack and discovered a thick, barbed fishbone stuck deep into the center of my foot.

Hospital.

Do not cry.

Novocain.

A few stitches.

We hadn't returned to the pond since. I'm not sure why, but the fishbone stabbing left everyone with a bad sensation and no desire to return. But my father was bigger than that, and his father had hunted with him, so it was time for me to do the same: a rite of passage into manhood.

Following the birds, I awakened a murderer: a man. And we went fishing, snatching, and roasting whole fish with spikes through the mouth and tail.

The fish tasted murky, as if we had eaten mud itself. "Add more salt. That'll do it." We tried adding more salt, but nothing worked.

The fog dissipated, leaving the fish meat mostly uneaten. Once home, the firearms were cleaned and stored, one gently next to the other.

Doves are put far into the freezer.

2023

My face is on fire; we've been driving for hours. I'm riding my prewar 1937 Harley-Davidson EL Knucklehead, the roughest hardtail available, and my body is already broken. A '47 Indian girder on the front provides some relief from the difficult terrain of any of these desert rides. However, this journey is physically demanding.

I came here as a youth. I spent a lot of time traveling with my mother, and subsequently with my children without her. My children are no longer with me, but it feels as if my mother has returned, albeit indirectly.

Back then, I'd be in the backseat, staring out the Cadillac's rear window at the distant electrical towers and brushstroke blurs of posted red-tailed hawks; now, it's similar but less charged. Then, on our way to California City, Mojave, or Truth or Consequences, New Mexico, I'd frequently spot a figure on the shoulder of the road—but there was never a side look, only a deadened stare straight ahead. And it was always "He." Men do that sort of thing. They abandon their families, gamble themselves into poverty, and escape from prison without a strategy. It's all on the same page: cruel, ruthless, and always carrying a backpack of terrible neglect on their back.

Even in this gale-force wind, I can hear several voices. I'm not sure who they are, but I hear, "Look in the mirror and tell yourself you're fine." Say that ten times every morning: "I'm okay." I'm okay. I'm fine." I'm not sure why I'm hearing this in my brain, but I am aware that it is today's status quo language. I can hear it directing a musical composition of its own imaginative, imaginary conception. These voices prey on the lost, but I am not one. I am surrounded by the constant soft wind of the "I'm not okay" generation, which is being battered by hurricanes of "fix it" debris.

Long-distance travel is not without its drawbacks. However, the impact of that pain should not be underestimated. The agony is there in the surroundings. It is working its way into the fabric of what will become our sense of self, our personality.

In a grid, we are thirteen strong. The rooster is constantly on my left. We are both in the front. I am on the right. We're heading to the Choppers Magazine Roundup in Virginia City, Nevada. It's a 1,200 mile round trip, and we have four days to complete it. We need to go quickly through the desert heat and hope that we don't break down. We're pushing our bikes between seventy-five and eighty. My right thigh is burning because the higher exhaust pipe was installed too high. At these speeds, the temperature is higher than usual, and I can feel it. My bones feel like they're being stripped over a campfire, yet we can't stop till we need gas. We can't stop till we have to.

I should pull over and wrap a shirt across my face. I can feel how red it is. It's ablaze. The outer layer is withering. It stings, yet something inside me smiles. I belong out here. I belong to a group of guys who seek personal validation in a mirror under a harsh midday sun on homemade pieces of technology designed to withstand a century. And just as that notion crosses my mind, my helmeted head crashes into a little swarm of bees I didn't see coming. They slap me like a flurry of miniature blows. I fumble around for a moment. The ache against my face's already hypersensitive nerves is worthy of tragicomedy play. I breathe through it. I take it. I won't pull over. However, the sting becomes more intense. It's unbearable. I suddenly hear George Jones on the radio and realize I'm on another desert journey with my mother.

I am now a child in the front passenger seat of my mother's automobile. She has her left leg drawn up beneath her ass-cheek, a fizzing Dr Pepper in the same left hand that is on the steering wheel, and a lighted Kool King in the right. Because of the little dust devils we pass through at speeds of over 100 mph, the smoke is sucked out the window at irregular intervals. Trips back to my childhood toughen me up, and when I relax into them, a sense of soaring returns. I am flying. I am practically out of my body, floating above the asphalt. My midsection is tight, but I'm used to it. I'm used to holding things semi-rigid. I do not think about it. Everything in me anticipates but remains comfortable. All the bikes next to and behind me are roaring spits and coughs in the same pitch. The pains in my neck and face have gone. It wasn't the pounding bees' fault. I am the one who is unnatural and foreign. It is I who is visiting with an ego, concerned about the impact I will make on this existence. But not now. Pain, no pain—I'm right here. I'm burned, stung, and in sync. We'll have to pull over eventually, but for the time being, I'm thrilled.

So, as a child, hand out the window, Mom driving us to a Whataburger a thousand miles away in Texas (just because she felt like it), I learnt to appreciate the raw, exposed flesh of the desert. I may have complained at the time, but I discovered that the thing that scared me the most was also the thing that would ultimately empower me.

I did not look in the mirror this morning. I mounted my ass on my bike and rode away with a group of dirty dudes to a place far away.

2004

We were drinking GRAPPA, which is formed from grape waste after the wine-making process and tastes like it. When you sip it and pretend to be aristocratic, you get a fiery mouthful of reactions; the bottom line is that you're drinking it to get drunk, so you just deal with it tasting like rubbing alcohol and being left as the post-wine-making waste product that it is.

I had rented a cottage in a little lake village in Italy with Paul Haggis while he was editing his directorial debut, Crash (which he asked me to leave since I added nothing to it). Italy has always piqued my interest, so what could be better than strange guests turning up at our party, staying for a few boisterous days or weeks, and then vanishing as quietly or noncommittally as they arrived?

Following one of the many nightly drinking sessions over those months, a few of us decided to venture into the Hessian maze of soot-swathed lanes to see what would spark. We ended up at a café one piazza over, talking late into the night under eerie tungsten street lamps, which seemed to satisfy our ghoulish desires. When we were nice and sauced-up, I told them a tale about my sixteen-year-old son who decided he wanted to learn more about Scientology, so he boarded a bus to the Celebrity Centre in Hollywood and took classes. He would phone me from such bus rides and tell me about the influence (or lack thereof) that this "cult" was having on his life. He thought some of it was practical and beneficial, but others were goo goo gaa gaa crap, as with other homemade religions.

It wasn't until Trevor advanced to the next level and was told he was ready to coach that reality hit him. "I was listening to a woman who had come in frantically. I was listening to her do all her dirty laundry when my mentor, who was sitting next to me, slipped over a small, folded piece of paper that read: 'Get a load of this piece of work: what a wacko.' That's when I knew I was out."

Everyone smiled as I told this anecdote.

Then . ...No grins.

What?

We are Scientologists.

...what?

Paul's wife pointed to Paul, who sat next to her, and then herself.

We are Scientologists.

What do you mean?

We are studying Scientology.

For how long?

Decades.

Decades?!

My face bled. I looked around at everyone else who appeared to have known the same thing and either assumed I did or couldn't wait to see me eat shit.

I apologize.

No! Not at all. That's a bizarre story. You have a son. That's crazy.

Yeah . ..I understand, right?

Yeah. Crazy.

We all sat there, calmly sipping our rubbing alcohol.

Years ago, I was asked to dinner with John Travolta; Kelly, his lovely and uber-pleasant wife; Marlon Brando; a redhead Marlon had met on the internet; my father and his wife, Barbra (a singer). I was twenty-seven years old, and the only reason I got into acting was because of the early films I had seen starring Marlon Brando and the late James Dean (who, incidentally, died in an automobile accident on the outskirts of my hometown of Paso Robles and ended up in the same morgue as my mother just months before his fortieth anniversary).

Wow. I was supposed to meet Marlon Brando.

Marlon arrived late for dinner, wearing a blue dinner jacket, loose slacks, and a scarf around his neck. I don't remember the color of the scarf, but I do remember how fashionable it looked. I'm going to start wearing scarves, I told myself.

When he got out of the car and stood up, he reached down to pull up his pant leg. Blood was pouring down his leg from beneath it. He claimed that he had stopped to assist several individuals in pulling their cars from a landslide on the Pacific Coast Highway. As he attempted to pull a car out of the muck, it gained traction and the bumper struck his leg.

"I just made it to the next level!" Travolta shouted from behind a bush, I think.

Marlon sauntered over to John, and John to Marlon, and they exchanged a cheerful hug. John joyfully told Marlon that he had recently completed a healing course and could assist him. John tenderly grabbed Marlon's hand and guided him inside to Barbra's living room.

When I stepped in, Marlon was lying on a chaise lounge, and John urged him to close his eyes. I stood quietly, leaving mine open.

John placed one hand on Marlon's calf, then the other on his chest. Time passed calmly. Nobody spoke. I was furthest from them. I was watching. Marlon Brando with Danny Zuko. This is ridiculous.

How about that?

Marlon opened his eyes.

Wow.

Right?

Yeah.

I understand. It's really something.

Marlon stood up, appearing less pale than usual.

Wow.

Right?

Another friendly hug.

Let us eat.

I had just seen John Travolta fix Marlon fucking Brando.

I should have shared that anecdote in Italy.

1991

I've had my first drink in three and a half years, and I've taken another turn. My brain feels like another entity, an engine designed by someone else.

I gaze at the beer. It hisses at me. It wants to save me. My emotionshave enslaved me, trapped on the hamster wheel of seeing my life slip away. But now I'm home, in no-man's land, and free to do whatever I please. Oh, these faces are passing me by. Nobody's staring at me. Oh, love. Where are you now?

I drink the foam. I am yours. Acid reflux rushes up my throat. My chest tightens. I open my mouth wider. I let the froth sit on my upper lip and let the liquid sink behind it, spilling into my mouth. I swallow and wait.

I swallow and wait.

I swallow and wait.

I swallow and wait.

Everybody is moving. I want to fight all of them. You've died!—All these dead are invading my eyeline. You know who you are! These disease-infested corpses trotting along: callous machines strolling the streets to and from their work schedules, sticking to imagined lifestyles through the molasses of their denial of what is and isn't true. Take a photo of me with my beer. I want MORE ALCOHOL; exploit me! I am free! I am free! I'll roam the streets by myself till the sun rises. I'll wander down the red-lit hookers, who are so young, and cry. I'll talk to them. I'll want to preserve them, then punish myself for being so naive. I'm so young! How did I get to be so young?! I live in the worst areas, don't shower, and puncture myself with smudged lead from broken pencils. I'm DRUNK! How did this occur? What was I thinking? Fuck you!! COME HERE! YOU! COME . ..HERE!!!! I run. I hop into a bunch of young lads, nice, preppy boys sipping wine spritzers. They kicked me. I swing crazy. I can't feel anything. Hit me. I hit you. You struck me. Blood. A bottle was thrown. I run. I turn one corner, then another. Cobbled streets. One light. Shadows. Another lone light. More shadows. Keep walking. Find another bar. Blood on the face. Blood on the hair. Homeless French. More alcohol. I will share. Share with me. Another fight. I fall into the Seine. I am cold. I don't recall where I live. I have a child. Eric Clapton's son fell fifty-four storeys by accident, according to reports today. I'm tossing. I am cold. I am moist. I am on the sidewalk. Where do I live? I'm terribly sad for Eric Clapton. I want to go home right now. My clever son, keep your heart. I really love you. I'm drinking. I'm drinking. Pull yourself off the sidewalk. Where do you live? Where am I now? Excuse me? Where am I now? Do you know where I am??

CHAPTER 6
BENEATH THE CANOPY

*I*t's late morning, and a canopy of trees protects us from direct sunshine. We'll marry in three days. Still in bed, awake and snug, with all of our pals trickling in: enthusiastic, inspired, and slightly unwelcome. I sat up at Mac's View last night, where we'll marry shortly after the sun sets behind the large granite boulder in the distance. I stood there and watched what remained of the sky slip away, taking with it any more soiled elements of my past that I might have been clinging onto.

The woods are very lovely up there. They only let the best light shine through a canopy of big leaves. I sat, watching the silhouettes of the military-straight trunks of trees remain firm as the wind shook and tickled them. This place is as mysterious as the feeling I have of marrying you so soon.

It's personal to us. We are painting the canvas of this wedding whatever we want. And our friends are nearby, the ones who took the effort to celebrate who we've become over the last several years. I need to give a speech about them. I need to write my vows to you and pull from the roots of who we've been, and the adventures that have been a constant for us, the times when the laugh won and the challenge of how to get a decent night's sleep without searching in the dark for yet another kiss: Costa Rica's dust and sweat; Greece painted white and cuddling in our hovel bookstore; riding bikes down the boardwalk of Venice Beach, waving and being waved to by all the local help-worms; surly neighbors yelli We are the symbolic fusion of Black Sabbath and Taylor Swift.

Today, in front of all of our friends and family, I swear to carry your dreams as closely as I would my own, protecting them as you work to make them a reality for you. I will love you as we walk side by side, taking those moments to pause and stow away to remember that we are here today to face this life together, to cherish every kernel of it, every hint of its aroma, and every skinned knee and bruised elbow that comes with it. We persevere. I promise to be there for you through it all: to hold, cradle, hoist, desire, lean on, whisper to, learn from, and always cherish our time together.

You are my best friend, and I promise to keep that in mind in whatever we do, just as I have since we met.

You are everything I am most thankful for. I am really fortunate, and I would be honored if you would accept me as your spouse as of today, and I assure you that my love for you will continue into the future.

My mother owned a watch like the one I'm giving you, and she was the most important person in my life. This is a representation of our timelessness. Each movement you make, the watch winds, and each movement you've made has impacted me tremendously. I adore you as you are today, and I consider myself extremely fortunate to be able to marry you.

Sincerely and with adoration.

Your husband in a few minutes.

1975

Every weekend when we were kids, especially on Saturdays, we'd get out of bed with great excitement. Whether it was a hundred-degree summer day or a dog-bowl frigid twenty-five, our spring chicken glow as we rolled out of bed was always visible. Saturday was Hoover's Beef Palace, and we'd put on our boots, Carhartt coats, eyes still swollen from sleep, a Ready Western hat, and drive down the driveway, watching the ground squirrels scurry away frenetically.

About halfway there, we'd start salivating at the notion of the tractor-dirty chef's buttered-up French toast next to the two gigantic eggs, the additional dollop of unnecessary butter, the two (what appeared to be) loaves of rye toast, and the small pile of well-done hash browns. We'd sit at the counter while those thick-armed country women carried ten-pound plates of compost gold from the kitchen to tables strewn with kids we'd just seen at school the day before, grandparents with dirty Band-Aids wrapped around at least two of their calloused fingers, and then there'd be a frenzy as we savored every morsel of our plentiful orders. Cowboy hats were the norm at Hoover's, and they were worn casually.

After breakfast, we'd stroll out the back door and over the dirt lot to the auction house, where we'd sit on wood-splintered fold-down seats and watch various cattle being herded in while the man behind the microphone rattled off sale numbers at breakneck pace. One cowboy would raise his hand briefly, then another would gesture, and so on until "SOLD!" would resound through the sales arena like a hollow echo, accompanied by the tight smack of a gavel. The woman next to him would write something in her spiral notebook, and a whole new cluster of cows would appear. We'd sit there and watch with a slight twist of anxiety on our faces because we knew if we raised our hands, even in a thoughtless moment of scratching our noses, we'd end up driving back home with an eight-hundred-pound heifer strapped to the bed of our truck; and with these boys, that wasn't something you wanted to get stuck with because there was no turning back.

Life at Hoover's sung to all of us, unaware that we would ever lose the tune. But the song has faded into a recollection of a time when adversity shaped character, and the resulting music spoke in a calming voice you never expected.

Country blood runs clean, and clean isn't what the world sings about anymore.

2001

RAMONA BECAME MORE MY BROTHER'S MOM THAN MINE, about 1974 to 1975, after we relocated to the ranch on California's Central Coast. My father was an actor and was usually around on weekends at first, then every few weeks after that. My mother, Jane, was preoccupied with animals, namely the health and well-being of wild creatures. She had spent her entire life with animals, picking up stray animals on the street since she was in her early teens. Jane had no idea what to do with the two newborns who ran in and out of her house at will, but every now and then we'd hear "Sic 'em!" from their gurgling lungs." and you'd know right away, that if you didn't get on the other side of that closed door within a few seconds, you'd be cleaning up fresh, red marks somewhere on your body for the rest of the day. They were not dogs. It'd either be a mountain lion, a wolf, or a cross between a dog and a coyote: a wild animal that someone had the foresight to remove from its natural habitat so that all their neighbors could gawk, praise, and envy endlessly, not realizing for a second that a wild animal was not supposed to be in a house eating dog food in the first place.

My eight-year-old brother, Jess, and I were dashing in and out of the home, our radars sharpened and our legs ready to outwit the most cunning of whatever predators were hiding behind a couch or a bed stand—but the chances were not in our favor.

"Sic 'em," she'd say, and a few seconds later, a faint yelp came not from me, as I looked down to my legs, expecting blood evidence, but from my brother a few yards away. Then a door slammed twice, once on the wolf and then again to reinforce the barrier between the beast and my brother.

"Why did you slam the door on Lefty?!?" she would exclaim.

". ..what?" A faint sound sounded from behind the closed door.

"WHY DID YOU SLAM THE DOOR ON MY WOLF!?"

". .."Because it was trying to kill me," Jess admitted.

"Kill you? KILL YOU? Love bites you, little crap! Love bites! Open the door!"

". ..no."

"OPEN THE DOORS!!!"

. ..click. (.. errrrrr eeeeeeee)

The rest is history, as they say. The rest is too graphic to write.

Ramona had scars on her butt and her tummy. The doctors discovered scars in her stomach and throat when she went to the hospital complaining of "inside pains." She had been complaining of "inside pains" for about a month, but it took my mother nearly that long to believe there was anything going on other than simply endless whimpering. Ramona had damaged the lining of her stomach from retching so much while cleaning up the armory of never-ending shit that stretched from the floor of the far end of our kitchen to the edge of my mother's bedroom door, which was always closed tightly. I would watch her from behind a couch, sometimes settling onto her knees with a few gathered paper towels in one hand and the lemon Pledge in the other, and there she'd be starting in on what then seemed a dismantling of landmines during a firefight that was happening along the lining of her insides—she'd bow her head away from the fumes so as not to disrupt this delicate danger before her: the hands would start to tremble, a few beads of sweat would fall down her va Then came the retching: the lips opening slightly, held together by a string of fresh saliva. Adam's apple would peak, the stomach tightened, the eyes lifted, the chin quivered, and the hands would extend and float in midair, as if suspended by a puppeteer. The pores opened and let free of the water held inside them, signaling that the disassembly had failed miserably—and then it would happen again, and she'd retch and retch and retch some more. I'd sit there, half hidden behind the sofa, feeling so bad that I couldn't do anything because my mother would come out, having heard the retching from behind her bedroom door, which interrupted the test-taping of country-western songs that she was recording with her screeching chalkboard voice, and there would be chaos—complete fucking havoc.

Ramona was our mother for 7 years. She left on September 4, 1981, sometime during the night I was thirteen. Jess was nine, and that was the last time I saw him, because he drove his personality into his brain's garage and closed the door. He went to see her on the outskirts of her hometown of Guadalajara a few years after she left, but he was never the same. She now has her own family: a baby boy covered in flies under a Swiss cheese roof that sat atop a modest pad of rough Mexican soil. He looked at her hard, quietly pleading with her heart to reunite with him. But she had her family, and our real mother had animals. Jess left. He left for good.

The door slowly opened, revealing Jess's small four-year-old eye.

Can I stay here awhile?

"Do you know what? You need to spend time with these animals if you want to be any kind of man when you grow up, which you aren't yet. Do you want to run away from every dog you see on the street or cry when you watch a little kitty cat stalking a tiny mouse?"

My mother's voice would break into song near the end, mocking the notion that he was a child with any sort of feelings, and I could see a tear falling from that one eye, which was now slowly glazing over.

". ..I am a man; I just don't want to come out right now. I have other things to do here. ..."

I'm not sure if he finished the sentence or not. He was murmuring a lot because he wanted to stand up to her, I knew, but he knew just as well as I did that if he did, he'd end up in a mound of tears and invisible bruises.

My mother was just five feet three inches tall. She weighed only 105 pounds and drank Calypso Coffees by the dozen. Calypso Coffees were created with "light rum, Tia Maria, with a little whipped cream on top, please," which quickly transformed into the nonsensical "lignum with a lil whip cream—AND DON'T FORGET THE." ..ummm . ..MARIA GODAMMIT!!!" No bar owner would ever eighty-six her because they knew, drunk or sober, she was still the same frantic, shit-kickin' bitch who'd find her way back in there, often with the protection of their clients. Nobody wanted to make things worse. Nobody knew whether they should love her or dispose of her body. I think they thought that if they did, if they actually took the muscle and got rid of her for good, that she would somehow make it back, just like in the bars, just like after every drunken eighty-miles-per-hour car wreck, she would somehow crawl out of that grave and haunt them again and again with insults they couldn't even imagine, dodging that bullfrog voice, which seemed to echo through county after county, always looking for a new stud to kill,

"YOU GET OUT OF HERE RIGHT NOW AND SPEND TIME WITH THE WOLF!"

". ..okay! okay! Just a second, I need to put on my shoes. .."

"YOU ALREADY HAVE YOUR SHOES ON!!!" GET OUT OF HERE!!"

She kicked the door.

"I need to put my shoes on." .."Just wait."

Then, from the same couch, I'd unhappily watch Ramona's attempts to wipe wet excrement off the floor, and with the worst sense of timing, I'd tell my mother, "Let me put his freakin 'shoes on."

She turned her head toward me and stared at me for a long time with those tired, animal eyes of hers, before finally, with tremendous constraint and disdain, saying:

"Fine, whatever you say."

2022

When I put her goggles on, she clutches them closely to her eyes. I smile and give a tepid snap to the elastic on the back of her head before slowly backing away in the water. Her already-there smile reveals how thrilled she is. I took a time to take her in: her golden hair washed an easy brown with highlights at the ends, and her feet had multicolored toenails painted by her mother before they crept into the bedroom to see me this morning for Father's Day. I look at her bathing suit, which zips across the front, is long sleeved, and has paisley designs that are confusingly imposed. Although the water is not chilly, I can see her mouth chattering. I wonder if her body is still unable to control temperature, as it was when she was a newborn. There is too much to recall. I check the color of her bottom lip to make sure it's not a frozen, bruised purple. There are so many things to keep straight, so many things that are there to be forgotten or whoopsie: feed, but no choking; toilet, but no sliding off the toilet seat; hug, but don't force it; say hello, and remember that being shy isn't a disease; sleep on the back, now on the side; don't run on wood floors with socks; we can pretend things are knives, but we don't actually pick up knives; pull over when you forget to buckle them into their car seats; hold their hands

Are you ready?

Yes. I am ready!

The smile grows wider. The teeth gnash. She takes small, exuberant steps forward, knowing I will not move but doing everything she can to prolong the anticipation of it all. I plant my feet.

Go!

I am going!

Okay, when you are ready.

I am going!

She shouts this as she leaps forward in a cycling run, landing in the water in the same frozen position.

I watch her swim toward me, twitching, writhing, and twisting her hips to gain as much momentum as possible. She extends her arms forward, but her legs stop moving. She kicks her legs, causing the arms to float limp beside her. I learned that when an arm reaches for a handful of water while simultaneously attempting to parallel kick, she short-circuits. It is a revelation. I experienced it as if it were occurring to me. She's 3 and a half. It's like patting our heads and trying to rub circles on our tummies. It takes practice. It is a taught skill. It can't happen right now, so we'll have to practice whenever we can.

The palm of my left hand lifts her from the pit of her right arm, and I bend down to hoist her onto my left hip.

Wow!

The smile.

Wow!

Her breathing is labored.

She's staring back at the distance she's traveled. Today's sun is really hot. It burns, but she can't feel it. She's still, but she's agitated in my arms. Her eyes are filled with craziness, and without enough recovery, she collapses, rendering any grip I have on her useless. Her head is currently underwater. Her expression is downcast. She twists and pulls forward, returning from where she came. The fucking girl is a machine. She's my machine.

1981

I can't remember what day it was, but it must have been a weekend. I was in Jason's temporary room against the garage on the wrong side of the house. It was the same room where, at the age of fifteen, I forced him to tattoo JB on my right shoulder with Indian ink using a primitive needle just above the scapula. That is all it said. Me. My moniker. My brothers, the Cito Rats. Rich Kids on LSD (RKL) hadn't started yet, but it would shortly. This was before that. We were all skateboarding and surfing together. This was taking a ride from Matt Mondragon's hunchbacked grandmother, Dee, in the blue, rusting Datsun 510 wagon with all of our boards roped and bungee-corded to the roof. Dee was our geriatric mascot. She was our main cheerleader with a walker, and she gave us everything she had willingly and gladly, especially her time. It was the late 1970s and early 1980s. This was when McDonald's was good for you, and hitchhiking didn't result in you being abducted and held in an underground refuge for seven years. This was the start of a whole new period of angry-adolescent LSD explorers, led by us locally, as well as the start of the cocaine frenzy, which none of us could buy and all of us would steal, fight, and fuck rich elderly ladies for. This was the time when the people I went out with flung full bottles of cheap gin at cops' windshields rather than fleeing. This was the era of the Herb Estate (an actual house where Mike Herbert and his single, drunk mother lived): a spray-painted middle-class home stripped of all its bourgeoisie and replaced with our rage, fueled by all the self-absorbed parents who would rather chew their respective ice than bother themselves with children; we built half pipes in their backyards and stole their cars while they were sleeping to go to the parts of town where they'd sell us cases of beer. This was before the drug epidemic, and Led Zeppelin was as punk as anyone who refused to attend fucking Woodstock. Sid Vicious was a hero, as was Darby Crash. Foolish Mortal, Herb, Dead Ted, No Hand's Dan, Bomber, Bohawk, Will Mo, T-Roll, the other JB, Twisty Mole, Mozz, Friend of Fat Chick, Hydro, Scott Doobie, T-Shaver, Hawkzane, Wookie Man, Chester the Molester, Dorbo, Galen, Horns, Car Ride Rick, Shark B, Razor Lips, and Fletcher, to name a few, were inside our destructive membrane. Then there was the Bottle Shop parking lot on Coast Village Road, where we spent a lot of time and were frequently detained. These were the years when we'd sneak out of town, ride in a van, and arrive at Godzilla's in the San Fernando Valley, ninety miles away, terrified, bloodied, willing, and smiling. The trips were well worth the introduction to a movement that felt as near to scrubbing a wolf's cage at seven years old as anything I'd ever known, and it was the best thing going on around us.

Every morning at five a.m., we would all wake up and ride our bikes out to Miramar Beach, whether there were any waves. We'd leave our bikes on the ground while it was still dark and walk barefoot along the railroad tracks to Hammond's Beach, arriving at first light. I'll never forget the burn on the bottoms of my feet when we returned to our bikes before school. It felt like a torch was aimed at them from six inches away. They'd be numb as they walked away from the water, but as they thawed, that irreversible anguish would surface, and no one would speak. During those heavy marine-layered mornings, we learnt how to deal with particular types of suffering. We knew what punk rock was before we could put a name to it.

That weekend at Jason's marked the beginning of our official Rathod. Jason had an acid sheet, a full sheet: one hundred hits. It was dubbed Red Rabbit and was famed for its heavy-headed but complex trails.

There were six of us present. His parents could have been at the opposite end of the house, but it wouldn't have mattered. Jason sported a permanent mischievous expression on his face. He was tall, straight-haired, blond, and lanky. You knew he was going all out; good or bad, he was eager to jump from as high as was necessary to ensure the most impact, and he was constantly discreetly wishing for the Hiroshima moment—we all were, but not as totally as Jason. The only other one who did this was Manuel Hyde, albeit for different reasons. Manuel was wild. He was intimidating. He and his brother were later killed in a gun duel in a field in Hawaii over a marijuana crop. According to what I've heard, he emerged from a makeshift cabin with a gun in each hand, possibly an AR-15. That sounded about correct. Last time I saw him, he had just gotten a cobra tattoo across his entire torso—a large venomous snake ready to strike—which felt like an omen, or a deliberate preparation for his end. It was the same for us all, but to varied degrees: we had no desire to suffer through a dead-eyed old age filled with regrets and wish-I-would-haves.

With the little paper square now like a piece of toilet paper in my mouth, I waited on the couch to see what happened. I was afraid. We'd all heard the stories and the myths, but Jason and a few others had tried it at a couple of punk performances and enjoyed it. With no idea what would happen and a brain that was only partially grown at thirteen years old, I sat there and imagined what my trip would bring, which paled in contrast to when the synesthetic effects finally showed themselves.

At first, the paths were as predicted. Then came the weight at the back of the head, like a monkey dragging on the base of your skull. Once things started, the monkey refused to leave. It kept pulling while I talked to the fireplace and then while I was outside watching the cartoon-laden tips of mountaintops break off, fall in slow motion, and stick upside down at their base (all without sound except for a cough when it landed, which came from somewhere I never quite understood). I raced nude down Featherhill Road at one point because I imagined it would take me farther into what was already a life-changing experience. Deeper. Anything to get deeper.

It was the most hopeful day I could have had. I not only survived the cave that transformed me from a boy to a man, but I also thrived. I arrived at what I hoped was the start of a happier life.

I don't remember seeing anyone else, but I know they were present. When I came down after twelve hours, just as the sun began to set, I realized that life was good and should be enjoyed, experienced, and tasted with a fully protruding, exposed tongue.

I'm not sure how we got from Jason's to Herb's that night, but someone recommended we do it again straight away: trip. It was a new rat mischief, and just a few of us had survived the previous phantasmagoric adventure. "Yeah" was all that was required. One guy said yes.

The Herb Estate's interior has been demolished. There were Cabbage Patch dolls placed feet first into the cork ceiling above, with syringes inserted into their heads. The brown shag carpeting masked all the dirt, stains, cum, and puke that lived there. "Ms. I had known Mike's mother, Herb, since I was eleven years old, when my mother relocated from Paso Robles to Santa Barbara on a whim. I met Mike when he attempted to run me over with a dirt bike when I was pulling my ten-speed up his road, which ran parallel to the street I lived on. He had wild hair, a gruff voice, and always appeared older than his age. He'd help us purchase drums or drugs because he could grow a Freddie Mercury mustache. The money for all of this came from my mother, who was one of the top five winners of the infamous pyramid scam of the period, from which few individuals emerged financially undamaged. I was her "counter," but she never informed me where she hid the money after I counted it for her.

She'd come in through the front door with brown paper grocery bags full of twenty-dollar bills, several of them, and walk straight into her bedroom, pouring them on the floor next to her bed and saying, "Count." She also kept an always loaded black 9 mm handgun on her bedside table next to the turquoise and pink southwestern lamp; there was a hit list, and she was somewhere in the top five. Then, one day, while she was away, I searched the home and discovered a loose board on the back of one of her wood drawers. Bingo. At least some of it. Overall, I ended up with around 6,000. With Herb's mustache and the gift of gab, we were free to indulge in our whims and wickedness at will. It was only me, Jason, and Herb at that point. That was the trifecta for years.

CHAPTER 7
SCREAMS IN THE HIGHLANDS

*M*y friend was having minor surgery, and I was there with my eleven- and seven-year-old children. We were visiting her in England. She insisted we travel, so we settled on Scotland. I'd always liked Ireland, but Scotland had never crossed my mind till then.

The Isle of Skye is a paradise. Later, I discovered that the majority of our ancestors came from the Highlands of the Isle of Skye, specifically Clan Ross and Clan Reed. Maybe it explains how we felt while we were there. The kids and I joked: "Where are we going to sleep tonight?!" I'd yell, and they'd respond in equal decibels, "We don't care!" We didn't care. We felt carefree and happy. We were members of Clan Brolin. We functioned as one.

Five days into our nomadic holiday, we arrived across The Quiraing, a landslip in the northernmost part of Trotternish, Isle of Skye, Scotland. There was no parking at the time, except for a little, damp dirt lot beside the roadside. Everything was new to us there. Everything was a discovery. Clan Brolin was just going along with whatever came along.

A trail was barely visible in the distance, providing a breathtaking view of the valley below. We decided to trek and indulge our whimsy.

No water bottle. We went off without knowing how long it would take, Eden, my seven-year-old, holding my hand and Trevor following after.

The hike was hazardous at times. It appeared to have shot down hundreds of feet from the trail's edge in a matter of moments. I questioned my abilities as a parent. What Am I doing up here? Why am I doing this with tiny kids? What about the typical playground? Why don't you follow the established procedures for children?

The trail would level off with the slope of the environment, and we'd be free to be our active selves.

Sheep are abundant in Scotland. They're everywhere, and this was no exception. Some of the mountainside was riddled with blue dots on white, while others had red dots. I assumed the colors sprayed on their thick wool denoted ownership: Farmer Blue and Farmer Red. Fine. I like sheep. So do my children. We've got sheep. They're cartoonishly funny.

"BAAAAAHHHHHH!!!"

I dashed at a group of them, my arms flailing. I expected my kids to laugh as they ran down one hill and up another. The sheep were terrified, but nothing bad happened.

My youth laughed at me more than myself. Our papa is insane, and I enjoy living up to the legend I perceive myself to be in their thoughts. We adore Crazy Papa.

I heard a snap just as I was turning back to face my children after stopping sprinting and waving my hands. I wasn't sure what it was. Then, when I refocused on the herd beyond, which was now rushing up a hillside, I noticed one of its legs dragging behind it, the front paws urgently scooting the body forward in breaks and starts.

"Poppy? What happened to that one?"

I jogged down to where the flock had been, and the lamb was still there, trying frantically. As I approached, it tried to run away. But it could not. Something was not working properly in its body. I hoped it was in shock due to the abrupt change in pitch. I hoped the sheep's body had temporarily spasmed and frozen.

I placed one hand on the back of its neck to soothe it, and with the other, I carefully pushed down the length of its spine. Vertebra. Vertebra. Vertebra. Vertebra. The sheep gave a cry. It was a cry of pain. We were two miles from our car. That portion of its back had collapsed. It moved. Something's broken.

I have spent my life surrounded by wildlife. Bobcats bit my cheek till it bled, and I've been cleaning wolf, mountain lion, and bobcat cages for as long as I can remember. I understand how to handle crises. I could have been a good soldier. Despite high levels of stress, I remain calm.

I looked over my shoulder at my children. They were staring at me, waiting for an indication on how to respond.

"Stay there," I instructed.

Please stay there. I do not know what to do. I was kidding. I was telling a joke. This goddamn sheep's back snapped. How the hell did that happen?! It was just a joke. What should I do?

But I kept my face on.

I looked around to see whether anyone else was on the trail. Nobody. I gazed up to the peaks of The Quiraing, where the fog was barely kissing the summits, and I felt the cold front of death penetrate my body.

The sheep moved slightly forward and bleated.

I gripped its body and tried to swing it to my shoulders. I could not. It was excessively heavy. I wanted to be the parent who could lift automobiles to save their children, but no matter how hard I tried, I couldn't.

I returned my attention to my children, who appeared sad and nervous yet stoic. They possessed the ranch kid grit that did not allow for an immediate reaction. They knew things were going to become worse, and reacting now would be premature.

"Turn your heads."

They did.

I could shatter its neck, I reasoned—one abrupt crack would put it out of its torment and pain. If I waited, would it be better? Where is everybody?!

I avoided it while I could. The sun was sinking lower in the sky, and all I knew was that I would have to kill this defenseless creature.

I gripped its muzzle with my left hand before bringing my right hand over the left side of his head and leveraging my left. I'll pull as hard and fast as I can, and it'll go out like a light. One. Two. "Turn your heads. "Cover your ears." They did.

One. Two. THREE. I pulled as every organ in my body descended into this hell of my own design.

"AAAAAAAA EEEEEEEE!!!"

The screams. The sheep kept screaming. Its back legs were splayed out, and it continued to scream as it reached forward away from me. It knew. It knew I was going to murder it.

There were no signs of physical trauma. None.

"Can we look?" My son yelled over his shoulder."

"Not yet."

I wasn't sure what to do. My children were watching me. This was a pivotal moment. There was no dignity in attempting to murder the sheep. There was just guilt and inadequacy. I wasn't sure what I was doing. I should know. I was thirty-one. I grew up on a ranch. I grew up among wild animals. I had to help in the deaths of animals in our home on a regular basis due to cancer, age, and injuries.

I placed my fingers around the nape of its neck. I said I was sorry. I apologized. I wasn't sure what to do. I had previously killed injured animals, including a stork on a seashore with a broken neck and birds smashing into windows who could never fly away again. I had also put my dog down when he was cancerous. I should know how to do it.

We were fifty feet from the brink of the cliff. I could throw it away, but what if it survived? I'm not sure what's down there. What if there's hay or soft bogs?

I looked up, and the other sheep were observing me from a distance.

My daughter was crying by now. It was a quiet, silent wail, only tears. My kid placed his arm around her. Ranch children console each other through all of nature's traumas.

But this was because of me. Do they believe that if I murder one sheep, I will also kill the others? Not now, but anytime in their lives? If I do this, would it always be alive beneath their skin, scratching at them?

I hauled the sheep up the slope as it continued to bleat and try to stand firm with its front hooves.

There were some loose stones. It was an old rock with a layer of mica and a hint of moss covering it. I took it, and two sharp edges were evident. I ran my hands over them. They were as sharp as they appeared. I imagined the sheep telling me to put it out of its agony, but I knew it wasn't true. It had no say in this matter. It was all in my head. The truth is that we were all dying on that landslip, but only one of us would die.

My objective. My aim needed to be spot on.

"Turn your heads. "Cover your ears."

My daughter wiped tears from her face with the back of her right hand before placing her palms over her ears. My son followed suit.

I lifted the rock above my head. One eye looked up at me from around my feet. The grass along the trail was a vivid green. I envisioned blood on it. I attempted to prepare myself. I'm a killer. I kill innocent people. I am not hilarious. There's nothing funny about me. Do not think. Aim. Save this animal from the anguish I have given it. Aim! Thank you, God. Please allow me to get it properly. I stand tall with the rock hovering above me.

1992

IT'S ON A WALL SOMEWHERE IN A STRANGER'S HOUSE, most likely purchased at a flea market years ago. You snapped a photo of me on my motorcycle, through a vehicle window with your friend, another monsoon of a lady. You brought it to me framed as a gift, and I threw it away in wrath. The next day, it was gone, a symbol of pure youth and passion.

We ended up in that shabby hotel room dead in the fire of day, all turquoise green and hot headed orange, when I slumped back, nude, in that swallow plastic bathtub against a discarded razor, slid down, and it cut a gum-stick-thick slice off my right shoulder. I didn't feel the pain immediately, but I noticed a murky red swirl in the water, like a blood dance.

And you sat next to me in that tub, straddling the toilet, brow furrowed, staring down at my feet. That was the standard look of an aspiring artist back then, when the desert wind was a constant fire that fueled our overactive sense of uniqueness and chaos; and as tortured as we were at the time, the story always becomes sadder afterward. We lived, for sure, but there was no way of knowing I'd outlive you. There was no way to know that. The look you gave me from that bathroom was one of grief; you knew I'd have a short, tragic life if it turned out that you died younger than you should have.

We had our time, though, in errant motel rooms and on long Harley-Davidson rides melting along in that age-old desert heat, evading frantic coyotes along the road and passing stoic hawks on fence posts at 90 mph in the delicious blur of a brushstroke.

I will miss you.

2006

I can't remember the room number, but they're all the same: Room 8 looks like Room 12 looks like Room 6—a queen bed, a pulsing plastic alarm clock, beige carpet, paper-thin Sheetrock, a sliding aluminum and glass door to the shower bath, small knobs on a small sink on either side of a small spigot. My hat rests on a cheap wooden chair, and my blue jeans stand out against the soiled flowery print of the bed's comforter. My boots stand alone next to the door, socks draped over the tops, as if they belonged to someone else. A film script is open on the small Formica table, describing a scene in which I hitch a ride with a stranger, who is shot by the bad guy the moment I jump into the truck and close the door with a metal-crunching slam. I don't work till it's dark tonight. Outside, it's hot. It's summertime. I hear high heels on concrete, so I pull back the curtain, and there she is, standing in front of me on the other side of the window. I unlock the door. Let her in. She doesn't even look at me, just passed past, wafting the aroma of aircraft food. She sets her luggage down, enters the restroom, and closes the door behind her. I hear the shower go on. My stomach cringes and contracts. I can feel the heat of the day behind me, and the heat of what lies ahead. I wish it was already nighttime. I wish my children were here. I wish I didn't have to do certain things.

1995

It began with me cutting off my thumb, which was the only scene I had planned with him. He'd grip my face, breathe in time with my frightened gasps (his idea), and walk away after handcuffing my wrist to an immovable object (I believe it was a pipe). That was when I hacked off my thumb in a fit of fear. Years ago, I recall spotting Nick Nolte seated at a café as I raged down Columbus Avenue after a disagreement with my then-wife. Our eyes locked in what appeared to be a future gaze for me. Now, years later, we were both present, staring at each other and breathing. I gazed into his eyes and couldn't see Nick at all. I just saw the man he was portraying, the role. This was a big boy school, with genuine performers and insane characters.

I was fortunate to obtain this film, as it was coming off of a Miramax run that began with Flirting with Disaster. Miramax deliberately discouraged me from working on that picture. I was a loser. I had never hit someone, but I was expected to. I had The Goonies, but that was a long time ago, and I hadn't done anything noteworthy since. I was beyond the point of rediscovery. But the director, David O. Russell, struggled for me. I was this figure in his mind, and although this was only his second picture, he battled tooth and nail to include me. Miramax agreed, but in return offered me nothing: no money, no credit, and no affection. It did not matter. I was used to it and glad to be there.

This was after that.

This happened when they liked me and believed in me. In essence, I was one of the "new guys."

I was afraid as I peered into his eyes. This was an actual actor. I aspired to be this type of actor. I wanted to lose myself in the roles. I wanted them to feel afraid and unsure of what I was going to do next.

He's dangerous, I imagined them saying. I accepted future accolades in the present. I demurred and raised my arm, clutching gold.

He went away—Nick: the legendary Nick Nolte—and I yelled the loudest, most venomous scream I could manage. I glanced at my arrested hand, attempting to maintain the state that I imagined someone facing death would be in. At that moment, I was objective and subjective. I was aiming to become a real actor.

CUT! Great. That was great. We received it.

I looked across to the filmmaker, a Danish man who had no idea that no one would see this film. But he recognized what was coming from me. He understood I wanted to be the best I could be with the legendary Nick Nolte.

I would like to do that once more. I've got an idea.

We've got it, though. That was great. You were excellent.

But, if it is okay with you, I would like to do one more thing.

He exhaled. He looked down. The staff waited for his response.

I'm twenty-seven years old, a drug addict on occasion, and half of my childhood buddies have died due to what our Cito Rats group became. But I was here, doing it in Hollywood. I was a successful person. I wasn't like the dead. I was breathing with Nick Nolte.

Nobody could deny that I was giving it my all. I could tell that some folks thought I was nuts. They did, however, enjoy this type of activity at the time. It fed into a mythos that was still popular at the time. Nick was one of the princes who cultivated such mythological significance. One more attempt. Proceed onwards. I've got an idea.

Okay. One more.

After action was called, Nick entered as his character, delivered the few frightening words of speech that were required, breathed with me, and then exited. I yelled again. I grabbed a knife. Cut off my thumb. I pulled my hand through the cuff. Hyperventilated. Shock. Fear. Relief. This is going quite well. I have evolved into the character. This is how I feel. Something I can't quite identify is dictating my actions.

I opened my tear-filled eyes. I was tingling. I was lying on the ground. I looked up to see a cameraman looking at me with curiosity and confusion. I realized I had passed out. I had lost consciousness.

CUT! Check his head.

What is wrong with my head?

You landed on your head. You have a large goose egg.

How?

We got it.

How did I fall?

I do not know. We need to go on.

Okay. Sorry.

All those years ago, the great Nick Nolte locked eyes with me on a New York City street and recognized an earlier self in my memory. I told him the story later, and he answered with a smile and a nod, which, based on my own experience with most twenty-seven-year-old performers, is muffled gobbledygook, like the characters in Charlie Brown listening to their teacher.

Nick saved my life later in the year. I was building a persona to live in at all times for this picture, and that character was so self-destructive that the human Nick Nolte felt forced to assist. We both fluctuated in terms of friendship and self-destructive behavior over the years.

But Nick Nolte was about to kill me, and suddenly he saved my life.

2022

I'm grateful for the two-by-three-inch portrait of my mother as a sixteen-year-old that sits on my desk. It reminds me to remember all the cremated creatures from our history that were burned and dusted within the wooden urns on the bookcases to my right, the most important of which held my mother herself. She shares it with Reggie, the chimp she lived with for most of the past seven years.

And I'm grateful for the rain, its consistency, and for going down beside the creek, which is too full to cross with a vehicle, so we're stranded here, on our ranch, happily. Our little angel daughter climbs up her first John Deere dozer in the shed, making vroom vroom noises as she pretends to work the gears and steer its wheel, while I watch my wife swing on the tire hanging from the tree that the monkey used to hang off and hoot from thirty years before. I am grateful for the phone call from my son last night as he gets lost in the hills of New Mexico, and I am grateful for FaceTiming with my older daughter as she plows a track through the northeastern snow with her dog and fiancé. I'm pleased that everyone appears to be precisely where they should be, including my mother on the desk here at the house.

I'm grateful that this is the only location I've ever wanted to live because I've been emotionally invested in its soil. I know the back roads, having walked and ridden them on horseback and motorcycles drunk and sober, in sorrow and ecstasy.

And I'm grateful to know what it's like to pull a newborn from a foaling mare, as well as to have known the wolves and coyotes of my youth who kept me company when I was too young to realize they shouldn't have as I quietly sat with them because what else could happen with a mother who only trusted those animals to instill something useful in my brother and me. We were only humans, and she didn't have much need for them throughout her lifetime.

It's not something that can be deconstructed until later, when I reflect on it with images of that maternal moon that has soothed me on so many despondent nights, or when old ranchers would come to visit with their fat-faced Chevy trucks and gawk when they saw a mountain lion chasing a small boy, my brother, across our dirt road. He never understood why he should not run away. He never received that. Perhaps I never did either.

1993

MOST PEOPLE ARE SITTING ON THE SUBWAY AS IT BANGS AROUND, BUT MY SON AND I STAND. It is rush hour, and we are in the thick of it.

My son is under the age of five, and he is holding on to the stainless steel vertical pipe that is bouncing up and down like an epileptic pogo stick. Everyone on the train is silent, but the snap and screech of steel echoes. I've noticed that people have somehow included ease into their natural algorithms: some study papers, others simply stare at the person across from them without emotion, and the majority listen to music on portable CD or cassette players.

There's a tap on my leg, and I look down to see him staring at me, as if he wants to say something but doesn't know how. I crouch down and grab the pipe for support. "What's up?" He looks down the other side of the car. I follow his eyes, only to discover a slew of individuals going about their daily lives. I quickly think he is witnessing a crisis: foaming at the lips, choking, water breaking, a young child being spanked. "What? What are you looking at?" "The guy," he responds. "Who? The guy. Him. There. He doesn't have a leg." I search the automobile and locate the man with no leg. He's a nice-looking guy with curling, filthy blond hair. One pant leg is full, while the other simply hangs there, like a brown newspaper stretched over the gray bench seat. I believe the dude noticed us (without looking over) talking about him. I'm sure it occurs all the time: secretly staring at the guy with no leg. What do you believe happened to him?Trevor murmured. Why don't you go ask him?Trevor looks at me as if I instructed him to go shit in someone's mouth. He was a bashful youngster, yet his curiosity would always get the best of him. "Should I? Certainly, you should. You want to know, right?He nodded his head. "Then go and ask him. I'm sure he'd be happy to tell you."

When Trevor becomes scared, he always goes formal. His gait stiffens, his torso rises, and his head remains completely motionless. As he paces over to the man without a leg, he never looks back at me, as most kids his age would.

The man with curly hair approaches him, listens to him, looks at me, and then returns his gaze to the still-under-five-year-old youngster. You never know what will happen in this situation. This individual could be insulted, get up, and scream or yell. The atmosphere here is dense with obvious fallibility.

I watch them closely to make sure they are ready. I can't hear what's being said, so my little guy turns around and walks back to where he was a moment ago, next to and under me, as casually as if he'd tapped my leg. When I look down, he is staring off into the horizon, as is the majority of the other passengers on the train. I glance at the guy without a leg, and he grins at me, which I interpret as a sign of respect: "You're raising a good kid, man." Good on you, says an imaginary voice in my head.

CHAPTER 8
THE HORSE'S MANE

*M*y brother and I sleep in two twin beds, both with slaughterhouse-red duvets. My mother refers to them as "the little brick beds." She comes in drunk some nights, sits on the edges of those large bricks, and asks us what she did the night before and why everyone is upset with her. Sometimes we tell her. Sometimes we don't.

Every morning I walk to the fence. I open the entrance to the horse corral and walk inside. One of them will inevitably progress. There she is, a mare, gently nuzzling my hand. Her whiskers. She pushes her lip back, revealing a layer of black soot along her top gum line. I grip her neck. I feel her breath, and her firm exhales brush across my face. I'm a child, slightly terrified of these intimate times, yet I wouldn't want to be anywhere else. I know not to walk behind her, so I touch her hindquarters to alert her to my presence. She's quite sturdy. I can see the muscles vibrating beneath the thin, taut red of her skin before she moves. I clutch her mane and hoist myself onto her back. She glances at me but does not move. I wonder if she'll take off running. I wonder if she'll try to show me that I shouldn't have mounted her in the first place? I wonder whether she understands what I am thinking. I am here to get out of the bedroom. I am here to evade these never-ending questions.

I tap her on both heels, and she gently moves forward. Her power is immense. She resembles the tractor we ride with Danny's grandfather early on Saturday mornings at the waste yard where he works.

We ride till we reach fences that we cannot cross.

My folks are like horses who may have fallen out of a trailer along a stretch of roadway on the grapevine and have since gone sour. My parents have a look in their eyes that suggests they might bite you at some point: one has a manic gaze ready to strike at any time, while the other has the same calm slow-stare as Lennie in Of Mice and Men. Both are harmful.

I've heard that a horse, if it hasn't soured, is a reflection of your faith in yourself. Parents are not like that. You must follow a distinct set of rules.

1992

Every day, she wore dirty white—an off-white blouse—and the heat from an open window on a usually humid July day made it translucent. He wouldn't look at her pants or her shoes, but the pants, he thought, were the type of polyester where the buttocks are firmly grabbed by the fabric in a continual squeeze, as in those old Life magazine commercials from the 1970s.

He had a little son at home and a sex-obsessed spouse. He'd write them extensive letters on postcards, twelve to sixteen postcards long, which they'd have to put together after they came at different times and were out of order. Email didn't exist yet. Cell Phones were heavy as bricks.

He spent most of his time alone, but he would occasionally venture out into the night, hoping to meet someone along the way. He was bashful, and he spent most of his energy contemplating how things should go in his life.

While he was there one night, he came across a small café deep in an alleyway he had never been before. His head fell as he walked. The dog poo on the streets assailed his nostrils, and the stench of unwashed men muddled his mind. Then, when hissing sounds from a heated espresso machine gave way to romance, he was dazzled by the aroma of her perfume, causing his feet to stop. He turned to see her, nuzzled in a corner of the café, white with a thin dress, hair up in a bun, eyes fixed on something on the table in front of her. He stepped in and took the closest available seat to her.

There was a lot of "as if" life back then, especially without alcohol; a wannabe writer who didn't comprehend language and only raped older women because he knew they'd welcome it, like a snapping turtle does a sprig of lettuce. He loved to wander in the dark, passing under the odd neon that warmed his head. The streets reeked of day-old beer and urine from the active urethras of the slaphappy, highly sexed dilettantes. And it lingered in the nose and lungs, like a glimmer of what the night may have given them, but not him. He just wanted to be involved somehow. He wanted his body to exist in multiple places at once, in all of the jars being shaken. He wanted to be publicly quartered and remembered as an appropriate adolescent romantic. He craved love without ever looking into the eyes of a lady who shared his quixotic yearning.

The woman in white sat there, sipping her coffee, as he began to write on the crude paper. The interaction between pen and paper sparked desire as it spun, describing the wisps in her hair.

He was too shy to consider what may happen if he stood up and told her she was lovely and he had no idea what to do with such beauty. That was too much for him to handle.

Later that night, he left, leaving his lover gravely behind. He entered the tiny door of his flat and quietly closed it behind him. He reached up and turned on the small TV. As the image slowly appeared on the screen, he lay back on his bed, adjusted his pillow, and listened to the weary French that he was still struggling to understand. The perfume of the woman at the café lingered. The grand romance with her, written in a journal on scrawled and warm pages, gnawed at him in small whispers. He rested his head against the wall, watching the black-and-white images on the TV fade in and out of focus until he fell asleep.

The next day in class, he believed he should know the name of the teacher, a French woman in her fifties who was doing her best to instill in her students the importance of learning French. She teed off a vowel, and it simply rolled along the pink of her mouth until it landed in its proper position. He watched her but never fully listened to what she said. There were other individuals in the room, but they didn't matter to him.

The teacher looked at him and asked him a question in French. He became frightened and felt the heat of his voice lodge in his throat. He looked down as she approached him and took his hand. She stunned him with her touch. His hand in hers kept moving, and he stretched his arm. It slipped under her dress, and the moisture on her skin called to him. He stared up at her, unsure what she may expect of him. She peered into his eyes and pulled him to his feet, and mischief reigned supreme in the room. The rest of the class stood up and marched out of the classroom in a single file, with the last person locking the door behind them.

She led him to the desk and turned to face him. He felt more at ease now, and he could look into her beautiful green eyes. She told him to sit at the desk, which he did. He could feel himself now, as she straddled his bowed, dangling legs. He felt more confident than he had ever felt on top of a world that was now his to do with what he had before been too terrified to take hold of.

The ink in his head took time to dry, and the words he caressed fell into the pages where his life was lived in a better bubble.

1982

ROCKY GALENTINE'S was the name given to a boisterous Italian restaurant that was more concerned with the display of an open kitchen than with the delectability of its food. It was a burning

Bikram-style theatrical Italian joint in Santa Barbara, California: a succulent sauna perspiring with competitive boners that served as our engines, while our little egos billowed into the great storms of laughter and taunting that reverberated through the little haunt on lower State Street until late into the early morning hours. It was a place to be your most adolescent self, and it still reminds me of that invincible mental state that saw adulthood as something only for geriatrics, and that without a bit of this ready-to-cum-at-any-second attitude, we were all doomed to staring off into a darkness of crushed dreams and unheeded adventures.

At the time, I was a prep cook and sometimes sous chef, making a variety of salads, tossing around some chicken dishes, and filling in for the head pasta cook when he was too drunk to appear. I smoked cigarettes and consumed Jameson on the fly. I chopped salads with the zeal of a heavy metal drummer and whipped the custard-based zabaglione dessert in a shouting, competitive fury as spectators cheered us on. I sliced the tip of my finger off while slicing bread, then lit my pants on fire with a pack of matches from my left jeans pocket. None of this mattered. I'd arrived, and I knew what I wanted to do with my life: become a chef. During the day, I was an emotionally clothed punk rock surfer who secretly listened to Journey and had revolving girlfriends who were just there for a minute before moving on to the next person, which none of my buddies regarded as inappropriate. The Cito Rats, as we called ourselves, were my misfit hive, and I was at the center of it: a collection of neglected children banding together in rage and need, with much to say but nowhere to put it. In summary, I didn't have much of a future in anything, but this seemed to suit rather well until I ended up in jail or in a terrible accident.

My fellow hornets and I spent the majority of our time before school, at lunch, and after school on a muddy slab known as The Gate. It was on the outside of the massive school grounds, which housed 3,500 students daily. One day, while we were down there pissing in the bushes, smoking out of empty dented Coke cans, or fleeing cops, I recall the tennis coach talking to his Izod-clad protégés, pointing with his overextended arm in our direction and obnoxiously bellowing: "If you want a meaningless life, just jog over there, and that's the group for you."

There was an old man at Rocky's with a white, well-trimmed beard who performed arias from great operas and would sashay from table to table while attempting high Cs. His voice was strong and friendly, and as tips came in the shape of shots and glasses of red and white wine, he stumbled along, enthralling those who came for the experience, if not for a great loaf of bread and some deep-fried mozzarella. And there was the caricaturist, who would charge guests to have their faces sketched in comical exaggerations on whatever vacant space left on the wall, which was already full of inebriated people eager to have their blackout stamped on the spot they would most likely forget the next day.

It was profitable mayhem for a while, and I was present. I went home with waitresses and partied with the older cooks until someone got into a fight or ignited a fire. I wanted to be there with these culinary pirates.

"Order now!!!" How it came in shrieks repeatedly moved me. The pans flew repeatedly, and the breasts landed sizzling. "Order now!!!" The shredded sheets of handwritten paper ripped off the order wheel, leaving shreds on the rubber matting underneath us. It did not matter what we cooked. It did not matter what they ate. The hedonism was in full swing. The circus was open, and the animals were being led out one by one, ready to leap on their painted circus stands and perform their acts.

It was everything to me, a life lived with such abandon. I expected it to last, but it didn't. The cooks, the servers, the sex, the tenor, the artist, the red and green stoplight reflections off the restaurant windows, the mayhem along Santa Barbara's longest mahogany bar, and what transpired after closing time all contributed to a later life I never expected: acting. Acting is simply a corrupted mirror of life in the guise of a condensed plot, with our lusts exhibited on a silver tray, ready to be consumed by anyone eager to spend their last dollar in the hope of escaping another lonely night.

2006

(Summer)

I WAS STAYING AT THE EL CAMINO (unfortunately no longer there, but replaced with a hipper, more sterilized motel with some other insipid current name like Inn on the Walk), when I was awakened by a phone call from my ex-wife, Trevor's mother.

The El Camino was a run-down motel located at the end of Las Vegas' main street in New Mexico. We were shooting No Country for Old Men there, largely at night. I had a friend visiting from a theater club in Los Angeles that we were running together. He was staying in another room that I had rented specifically for him. The only other person I knew who was staying at the motel was Keith, our prop master, whom I had known for years, and our desire to keep things dirty, nasty, and down-to-earth was similar. Nothing happened in that motel, yet there was an unsettling feeling there. It didn't matter if it was a death from years ago or current shenanigans—you knew the setting defaulted to terrible luck before good luck.

The phone call arrived a few hours after I had fallen asleep, just as the sun was rising. We had worked all night, with me firing at Javier's persona and him aiming at mine.

I rolled over when the rotary phone clanged.

"Hello?"

"Somebody just came over. Police. "They can't find Trevor."

"What does that mean?"

"An officer came over at 5 a.m. Do you know where your son is?type of thing. He was out yesterday night with a pal. I called around to various hospitals. They took two burn victims last night. They do not know who they are. "They're taking dental impressions."

"Are you saying that it may be Trevor?"

"I don't know."

I put down the phone, and my entire body shook. I had no control over it. I began to experience images about what it was like to have a deceased son. This cannot be. Not my son. When my son was four, I took him on a "happy face trek" through France, from Nantes to Dijon. We laugh together. We laugh all the time. My son adores me. What exactly do you mean by "burned beyond recognition?" I know exactly how my son looks. He's my son.

I called as many Los Angeles hospitals as I could. Everyone had someone who had died. Dead people began popping up, and I was curious whether any were my son and his friend.

"Can you look?" Could you find out? I can email you an image of how he looks."

"Hold, please."

I phoned another hospital.

Then another.

Then another.

Where was my son? Is he a burnt corpse sitting there, waiting for someone to remember him?

"Hold, please."

"Hold, please."

"Hold, please."

MY SON!!!

I conveyed the issue to the ultimate hospital, where he may be. "Hold, please." I knew I'd be contacting random hospitals after that, frantically hoping to see my son and laughing.

It was around five minutes before someone else answered the phone, and five minutes in purgatory is five long hours of something scarcely comparable to the time we've grown accustomed to.

"Hello, this is Dr. ____."

"I'm looking for Trevor Brolin, my son."

"Who is this?"

"It's his father. I'm in New Mexico now. "I am working."

"Hold, please."

This time, it wasn't as long. Another doctor came on and quite calmly—as if already recommending the death of my son—said,

"Is this Mr. Brolin?"

"Yes."

"Your son is here."

I instantly saw my son's remains. I found him in a drawer, blackened, exactly as the first hospital had described.

"Is my son alive?"

Pause.

"Yes, he is."

"Is he injured in any way?" Is this an accident? Is he okay?"

"He's fine."

"What does that mean?"

"He was inebriated. He is sleeping it off. Alcohol toxicity.

He was the only one who had been admitted, with no friends. A youthful night gone too far. Son of a well-known alcoholic.

As I was speaking with the doctor, little did we know that Trevor had awoken and, in classic Brolin fashion, dismissed himself from the hospital by just walking from the bed out the front door, wearing only green hospital pants, no shirt, and no shoes.

He strolled down Wilshire Boulevard with his shoulders open and his face to the sun. He was late for work, and when he arrived he had second-degree burns.

"I'm sorry for being late," Trevor bemoaned.

They stared at him, bowed their heads, then dismissed him.

I spoke with his mother about that time. Our youngster was awake and hungover. Our son is growing up. Our youngster is playing with the fire that I started in him.

I thought death had raped us for almost 45 minutes. Yes, we were raped: unwelcome, violated, and torn up insides. That's how it felt. I shook uncontrollably. All self-consciousness vanished. Family means everything. It has always existed in me as a white blood cell, protecting me from the rest of the world. My family has always been a positive force in my life. The world varies arbitrarily, neither good nor harmful. Nature assaults, then caresses. People come and go. Life begins and ends. But I'd always assumed that midlife crises were reserved for others. With my mother, life was chaotic, but with my kid, the pressures of being accountable for something so important to me meant everything. It arrived after that phone conversation, possibly for the first time in my life. There's no reason for my son, myself, or anyone else to be here. Life hangs on a shaky silk thread in a fragile web. We're in a marathon, and there's no clear finish line.

When my son was sixteen, we crossed what seemed like a line, but it wasn't a finish line. I know it's there—all of ours—and it'll be obvious once we cross it, but not until then. ...2020

AT THE PLAYGROUND TODAY, a man goes by with a little portable tape deck in his pocket while I am lying with my sleeping newborn, who is wrapped in a fleece snowsuit. He is playing a Native American prayer, which everyone can hear. When I hear the chanting suddenly overrun the few shouting kids and far-off leashless dogs, I look up and across to see him, slouched with dirty raven hair hanging down to his belt line, plodding by. My daughter stares at me, and I return her gaze while keeping him in my peripheral vision. The temperature has dropped in the evening, and there is still a cold in the air that was not present just a few minutes before. People are getting up from their covers, rubbing their hands together, and ending discussions about divorce, back issues, and new healers they discovered over the summer. Every lady looks like she went to college on a softball scholarship, and every child appears to have been conceived by accident.

And I return my gaze to the Indian, the chant dissolving into the breeze now, still bent and shuffling, and I recall a shaman I used to know who was ninety-five years old and laughed a lot with his thirty-four-year-old blond partner. I'd sit in a tent with him, hot rocks hissing, lungs singing, head swimming, and he'd be looking at me, smiling, still smiling, always smiling. I'm sure he banged that young ingenue frequently. You could tell by how she stared at him.

People are leaving, including the shuffler, whose music fades with the wind. My daughter has yet to unlock her eyes from mine. I can see the chill on her face as she shifts her focus to me. I know I will see that man again. She's still staring at me, as if she knows something I won't find out for a long time, as if the cold that has arrived contains something I can't detect. I envy her sensitivity, that darkest region that talks only in feelings.

1974

I'm waking up. We're at a smaller motel than the one we were in two days ago, and I can hear the crunch of someone going outside, possibly a worker. A car whooshes by, and my head pushes against the wall.

They should slow down.

I'm sure there are more youngsters here besides us.

Light shines through a small opening in the drapes, letting me know it is dawn. Daddy is still asleep, as is my brother, who is lying on the floor with my pillow. He says he doesn't like soft surfaces, so he sleeps on the wood flooring beneath me.

Daddy says he wants me to write every morning. He says I should write down my thoughts on a piece of paper, but he also says I can draw a picture instead if I wish.

He states he wants to know more about what I am thinking.

He claims I frequently stare off into the horizon, and I believe he is concerned about it.

I'm not sure why.

Something smells here. Perhaps there's old perspiration on the mattress. I'm not sure how many people have slept on this bed. It's disgusting to think about.

Daddy and I have to share a bed at times, as do the rest of us, but my brother invariably ends up on the floor. I occasionally get my own little bed, while they share a small one. It's funny because one of them falls on the floor during the night and then gets upset at the other, but I always chuckle with my hand over my mouth. Nobody can see anything because it is dark.

However, it is already morning and I am hungry. We ate at the petrol station last night: microwaved burritos, three Fantas, and three M&M packets. We sat on the curb, paper towels in our laps, and watched folks outside Bando's, a bar across the street that sounds like a clown to me. I was anticipating a clown to stroll outside, so I kept forgetting to eat. I don't like clowns. I like unicorns.

I wish they would wake up so we could leave. Maybe I'll turn on the television. I wonder whether this one works. I'll lower the sound all the way down to avoid waking anyone.

CHAPTER 9
TALES FROM LOWER EAST SIDE

*I*t usually begins shortly after being away from home. The job arrives, and you are consumed by the mystery of it. Then you get there, and it's pretty much the same: performers wondering where they are in the grand scheme of things, comparisons, loads of diversionary humor, and a few witticisms in moments of discomfort. After a few weeks, you begin to think of home, your block, the people who nourish you with their sandpaper personalities, and a culture that owns its misfits and celebrates personal monuments: Venice-Fucking-Beach. Every morning, I see a guy juggling a tennis ball, a bowling ball, and a chainsaw on the boardwalk off Windward Avenue while looking for a coffee handout near the Sidewalk Cafe. I do not have a job. Then the expected pervert tries to get me back to his apartment, which I will punch in the face before riding my skateboard along the bike path, jazzed up just enough to get me through the day.

Winter offers the oddest light, and as I look out toward the ocean, that gray-black wall creeps forward without suddenly, and everything descends into a scarier level. Everyone who lives here is aware of the ominous Bermuda cloud of Venice Beach off the boardwalk, which appears when things become just a little more severe and all the tourists go home, leaving the locals to feed off one other's ferocity. We are what the Lower East Side of New York was, combined with the worst of what Florida has always been.

I shall never leave this depth in the sewer of what will always have "original" emblazoned on its back-alley asshole, and where you can always get a greasy piece of pepperoni and a medium Coke for a buck and a quarter. As you eat it, a stray will ask if you have a can of spray paint because he just got an idea—and I'll know I'm home: that all of the other stuff is just some Nobu fantasyland smut with a small slice of jalapeño on its sushi and a roofie sitting patiently in some yuppie's nonalcoholic beer.

2021

Everyone is still asleep, and I don't start work until 6:00 p.m. I am meant to work all night. The children have been unwell with a terrible cough. It's desperately grabbing for me. I've managed to avoid it thus far, but I have a tickling sensation in my throat. Six o'clock is approaching too rapidly.

Dune was released internationally just over two weeks ago. The second half of the book is expected to be shot in Jordan and Budapest in June, with the possibility of shooting outside of Abu Dhabi. After that, we'll most likely continue with another season of Outer Range in New Mexico. A couple of years of hard work and a couple of years of losing out on what I've grown accustomed to— waking up every day to the ups and downs of being a full-time father. ...again.

The youngest can now stand on her own. The squat-to-fully-erect lift is almost impossibly easy for her, and she usually does it with a pleased smile, wobbling on what appears to be an imaginary tightrope. I frequently project the future of her life and what's to come: running with great abandon with her sister in the yard, dresses flapping in an easy wind; over consciously waiting to be picked up from school, boys watching them as they look out for our car to round the corner; the anxiety of homework and all the sounds, grunts, and attitude that come with it; the pride of graduation; first job; moving in, the words: "I love you Papa Bear" still coming from her just on the verge I see everything in a white flash.

This first year has passed so swiftly. That one-year-old smile permeates even the toughest armor. Her heart has more capacity than I will ever have. Everything is felt in her embraces and gaze. Her touch, both tender and fierce, softens me.

Her three-year-old sister carries an innate awe around the bingo basket of her mind, weighing, comparing, and quantitatively measuring the magic of it all before climbing it, basking in it, befriending and rejecting it. She is a woman who moves.

Sister and sister. They are a formidable duo. They sing through what has evolved into a new instrument, and the song is perfectly calibrated to what my ears prefer: music that touches my heart in the same way that Yo-Yo Ma's cello or Pavarotti's arias do. And, putting away all the romantic nonsense, their personal ties: strong, smart, daring, adventurous, crazy, humorous, creative, emotional, sensitive—as well as those distinguishing characteristics of ownership, respect, and a lack of pandering to others—serve me well.

To be blessed with these three daughters and a boy is beyond gratitude. It's as if a spiritual intervention knocked the ego out of my self-centered adolescence. Every couple of years, I am reminded of some Italian life in my seventies, complete with books, chess, wine, and young beautiful women slowly making the sign of the cross on themselves in front of a Medici fountain as the perspiration of an August heat wave caresses their cleavage—but then it passes.

We love each other. We try.

I nourish my wife with the tremendous love I have for her. Our house bleeds with the knowledge that we don't live by any manual prescribed by anybody other than ourselves, and that God may be in the process of shaping whatever we become.

So tonight, I sigh and reflect on all the undeniably damaged and dented years.

I rolled vehicles, plunged through windows, evaded cops, and fucked women I'd normally be frightened to approach. It was careless and unsafe. I endangered myself while abandoning others. I was pleasant until I wasn't—"Shark eyes," my friend T-Roll called it: "In the snap of a millisecond you went from charming to dark." The next morning, I'd lie there, crawling through the black molasses of my memory, anxiously looking for some proof of what I'd done the night before. I'd wake up on the sidewalk, knowing that I'd been too wet-brained to figure out how to go into my house and had eventually succumbed to the cold concrete. But it was worthwhile at that time in my life. Otherwise, I shivered with fear. I was trapped by what I believed others saw in me: nothing, an invisible, worthless word, and having anything like character was a valuable weight in this hell. I was all about myself, and no matter how much care, concern, or beneficence I showed, it all came down to servicing me.

Now, in my fifties, I wake up knowing where I am. My windows are open, which I recall doing last night. I am naked, and I recall taking off my dirty clothes and dumping them in a hamper that I purchased the other day at Budapest's equivalent of a Hungarian Target. I wake up with wide eyes, and while I don't need coffee, I appreciate the process. I'm exactly where I should be, totally conscious, and shame no longer follows me like a reluctant puppy being tugged on a leash. With this clarity comes an interest in smiles and genuine laughing, and the patience to suck nutrients from all the different walks of life that now tickle my fancy. Morning has me in its grip, and I'll walk today, to the river, up the hill, or to a coffee shop, to see and participate.

The world is a harsh, merciless dark alley. Sometimes a bar fight turns into a shared heaven that we never expected.

For the time being, I'll marvel at my luck.

Amen.

2002

I went to prison visiting Beaumont, Texas. I lied and claimed that I was researching a role or writing a play, I'm not sure which. The fact was that I really wanted to get in there and talk to the inmates, learn more about their experiences and how they dealt with both confinement and their relationships with personnel.

We became friendly after discovering that the warden was also sober. He gave me access that I would not ordinarily have had, and staff colleagues seemed to like me as well.

Bubba, one of the guards, handed me a photo taken by his mother during their backyard cookout. He told his mother, "Mama, fetch the camera so you can get me knocking old Grayson here right on his ass," and she answered, "Hold on. Do not do it yet. Wait!" as she dashed into the house to retrieve her camera. The shot was mid-hit, and the individual being punched knees were already bending.

It was a brilliant shot, and the fact that the mother took it at the son's request with no surprise or reluctance said volumes to me. I enjoyed it there, but it was backwoods crazy fun. As an outsider, it was fascinating to watch, but as Hunter S. Thompson discovered when he was hanging out with the Hells Angels, dive too deep and you may never get out.

I also viewed a video of a stabbing that had occurred in the prison a few years ago. They had a few of them, but the one that sticks with me the most included one prisoner rushing his own cousin in a recreation cell. The victim was going to be initiated into a rival gang, and six weeks before his release, his own cousin was assigned the task of snuffing him out.

He was stabbed 132 times in his abdomen. I could see him holding his intestines. At one point, he was more concerned about keeping his guts in than with fending off knife blows. What stood out was how long he stood. It lasted minutes, not seconds.

I've been stabbed once. Knowing that you may die is a revelation. You consider the most important aspects of your life at once, including the reasons you desire to live. The romances of a special life fade away, and you are suddenly enveloped in a blanket of humility, with the simplest things pulling at your heart like water does for a thirsty dog.

Watching the film, I witnessed the entire course of that young man's life lead to death. I witnessed the moment he realized he no longer had control over his future. He was numb, I understood as I watched, since the anguish had passed, and the simple act of holding on to whatever slippery membranes kept him alive was all that mattered. I noticed the despair in his eyes. The camera was very close. The guards couldn't go in until there were enough of them on hand to protect the area, so the stabbing continued unabated.

I often reflect on how my life has taken unexpected turns, and I am certain that there is nothing that separates me from what may have been. I keep it inside me, exactly the way the inmate did: on the point of falling out, on the verge of no levity at all.

2015

(Death)

He entered the chapel through the black snow. It was small, with numerous candles burning quietly. A painter's hue permeated the space, and as he stepped in, holding her hand behind him, a tear streamed down his cheek. It was his birthday, and they were high in the Italian highlands, in his favorite setting: a chapel.

Before he met her, she knew that only his children were important to him. Women came and went, and love existed for a time before fleeing, much like a short assault or burglary. Children cannot run because they are bound by an inescapable bloodline. She adored something about him. She realized that children and their parents were set for life, whether she liked it or not.

Birthdays conjured up images that he disliked yet, as it turned out, usually surfaced anyhow. However, chapels have always provided a sense of serenity. They were personal and did not need to exist, but did. The little societies that desired social intimacy required it. There was no gloom here: the chapel provided genuine relief, since those tucked-away holy shanties symbolized something loftier than the pettiness that people frequently resorted to.

She remained close to him while he considered his reaction. He turned to look at her because he could feel her smile and wanted to return it, for she stood there proudly putting this together just for him. It was his special day, and all day she had sputtered and hiccupped through so many sharp moments of suspense, praying her plan would work, crunching giddily through each dangerous step across the snow-covered forest. She led him, having walked it several times during the day, counting each step loudly as she went, knowing it would be dark when the time came. He trusted her and she felt stronger than ever. So he followed the subdued sounds of her left and right feet, delicately placing them where hers had recently landed.

The heat as they entered was romantic. The wind blew the trees outside. Snowflakes flowed softly down from the pine needles and danced beyond the chapel windows. He walked past the few blood-brown pews and up to a dazzling altar with a golden cross. Looking at it reminded him of his mother and the night the phone rang. The fury he felt at her departing his life, and the countless times she had made him smile, made him cringe and suffer. However, after a laborious reconfiguration, he smiled again.

Chapels existed in him, just as they did for the residents of the small towns that were around them, and she was aware of this. With each chapel they entered, knelt down, and held hands inside, something in them grew closer to each other.

But on his birthday, on his mother's death day, this chapel landed in his heart and flourished, staying there for years until it was time for him to depart.

Now, in the same chapel she had taken him into so many years before, she rested her warm hand on his cold one as the candles burned as brightly as they had before. The golden cross glowed stoically and dreamily where it had long ago. She knelt to say farewell and gently pressed her lips against his, knowing that he would have appreciated that it was still here, in the chapel they both adored, where they would spend their final minutes. It was as if they were back together for the first time: completely joyful, and for a brief period without even death standing in their way.

2021

This morning's overcooked and stale green chili apple fritter was strangely palatable. I ripped out chunks of it from the warmth of inside my van with a snap and dipped them into my coffee to help these frail getting-older teeth along. The apple came first, followed by the chili bite. I am not at home, yet here is my current home. I wander.

Earlier, we were blessed with prayers from some members of New Mexico's Native American community because we will begin shooting shortly, which means a lot to both of us. ..parties: we stand in the mud beside a horse corral, cowboy hats at our sides, and there is some urban stillness in the air, but it is fading, quietly melting away or disappearing with each new blessing. A sobering breeze whispers against our superficial hardships, as this New Mexican poverty that is everywhere yells at your seeming current states of affluence—as you attempt, as you try.

We've been waking up in the mornings to beautiful blues and pinks on the horizon with small wisps of snowflakes, and my instant want to go outside to feel the cold shock on my face and listen to what the morning has to say takes precedence. A drop of Copenhagen hidden beneath my lip gives me a little buzz. I grab my rope and look at my dummy steer as if he's already attempting to flee, then rope his plastic horns again and again until my hands grow cold and the ache in my fingertips yearns for the warmth of an over microwaved mug of bitter coffee.

I walked directly into the mountains yesterday, as something familiar began to return. I recognize this dirt. I've been here before, with other people, telling different stories, and waking up in bed remembering your face, whoever you were. I'm the same old guy, just getting older and more capable of appreciating the humility of being here at all, wherever at all; I can still wake up in bed and stroll through my memories before it's too late. It's what I'll miss the most when this is all over: journeying through such memories with nothing but quiet to accompany each phantom breath, when sounds normally vanish as quickly as they emerge.

The prayers conclude, and the Indians walk to their trucks, sort of waving goodbye. We stroll back to our horses, seeming to understand what to do.

2009?

"MY NAME IS BARBRA," she remarked to me as she extended her hand. Actually, this is a falsehood. I can't recall the first time we met. I'm horrible at that. I can't recall the first time we met, but I'd heard about her from my mother years before.

"I'd wanted to have met your mother. "I believe we would've gotten along," she murmured, invitingly.

"They would have loved each other!" My father exclaimed.

My mother had met Barbra in Sun Valley, Idaho, years previously. They were both visiting Clint Eastwood's house, which he owned. My mother had known Clint and his then-wife Maggie since she ran out from Corpus Christi, Texas, at the age of nineteen. They were the first people she had met. I believe that was in 1958, right before Clint got Rawhide.

"I think you guys have met."

"No."

I recall seeing a photo of them all together and my mother telling me that Barbra was harsh.

It did not matter. We've spent decades extolling the virtues of their union. In actuality, they would have despised one other. I'm convinced of it. Tough individuals nearly always despise other tough people, unless they have let their guard down.

But I've always liked tough women. I'm certain it's an Oedipal phenomenon. So, the next step was to get rid of my father.

No, I liked my father, so that was not an option.

She was my pop's girl, and we were all going to live happily ever after. That was it. That was the ticket.

Well into our happily-ever-after, I walked into their house one day.

"I'll have a glass of wine," I replied.

She stared at me and cocked her head, so I repeated myself.

"I'll have a glass of red wine, please."

She took a slow breath and nailed me with it: "Aren't you an alcoholic?"

That was a bold statement to make. Yeah, I'd known her for a long time; she was now my father's wife, and he was madly in love with her, as I could tell she was with him. "Aren't you supposed to not drink?"Man, there it is again. She would always wash her mouth with a bullshit cleaner before speaking with me. My own mother was like that, so it didn't immobilize me, but since she was no longer alive, this would have to suffice.

"It is fine. "It's only a glass of wine," I tried to explain.

"I don't think you should drink anything, right?"

She traveled all the way to Prescott, Arizona, to see me a few years ago. I was landscaping at the time. I'd quit acting. Fuck acting, I had rashly determined. I had already sworn off television (I despised the pace) and was trading stocks for a living, so I didn't need to act. I was raising two children, dealing with a ranch that had been given to me with no payment on the loan that built the house, and drinking.

"Hi!"She hugged me." I went out of the Prescott residence into the parking lot and into the hug. Then I hugged my dad.

Why don't you tie your shoelaces?I gazed down at my long, uncombed hair. I didn't tie my shoelaces since I was still determined not to do anything expected of me. It began and will conclude with no crap from her. It's what I've always valued most in others, no matter how much of my own enemy I was.

When a group of friends walked into the apartment I was staying in on Vineland Avenue in Hollywood, I was twenty-nine years sober. The El Royale. I'd lived there for a while, and my kids were either down there or up north at the ranch; most of the time, they were with their mother. I tried to keep everything separate from what was important to me: my children. However, those ideas will surely fail because they are focused on whimsy and reactivity. They have no real foundation. So the whole thing falls apart when the need arises, and booze, the great puppet master for me, takes control.

"It's just wine." You don't have to get it, but I'll take one later. So why not have it now?"

It's a conundrum, the psychology of winning, regardless of the costs. All I cared about was getting what I wanted.

I'd gone to jail several times by then. I had put my children in peril. I'd lost relationships and friendships. I understood that having a drink would not make everything better and would almost certainly make the issue worse.

"I'll get it myself."

"No, you shouldn't drink."

As with many in-law relationships, things began well, deteriorated, and then improved. My mother had died, and no one was going to replace her, no matter how poisonous she had been.

She once signed a card for me: "Love Mom." See, there it is. Mom. You're not my mother. You are my stepmother. Who wants to be a stepmother? Nobody. It connotes wicked intentions, such as drastic compensations for cosmetic inadequacies, misery loves company, and the me, me, me, syndrome. She was not that. She desired a family. She was being kind.

"I'm an alcoholic but I like red wine."

"You shouldn't drink."

"Do you know that?"

Yeah.

CHAPTER 10
THE FOREST OF MY OWN CONSTRUCTION

As I walked through Père Lachaise Cemetery with a baguette, soft cheese, and a few bottles of cheap red Bordeaux, I imagined myself as an urban cowboy and a hypersexed Joycean curiositor. My mother would have been proud. I imagined myself as a part of a society that thrived on adolescent tornadoes and oversexed Anaïs in wet dreams.

On one of those hot summer days, I met a young woman who was even younger than me. She was leaning on Molière's grave, feet bare, hair falling lightly down her face. She summoned me by sending her girlfriend to where I was standing. I had studied the language, but it did not come naturally to me. I stumbled through a few French sentences—something about the leaves and whether she was aware that Oscar Wilde was nearby—and we were soon in her flat, myself on top of her and her on top of mine.

Sex was normally brief, but kissing may endure for hours in those days. As a guy well into his gray years, I smile in retrospect at the memories of when there was no self-control and kissing was the superior alternative, especially in France, where the art of kissing and foreplay is still valued.

Where was the girl now? I cannot help but wonder. Those aromas that appear at odd moments, such as old vinyls, dirty dogs, perfume that peaks the nose, and/or day-old cigarette smoke in a bar about to open. All of them are random, yet they desire for a more comprehensive picture.

I'd never want to go back now, to be one of those fifty-something-year-olds trying to catch up to the younger ones, anxious to be heard, appreciated, and imagined great by the unshowered few. No, I'll settle for my recollections of daring experiments that led me precisely here, in the forest of my own construction.

2008

THIS MORNING IS QUIET, and it is the only time it has been so. Pigeons are all I hear. The only other thing is the tongue and groove sounds beneath the tires as they roll and skip by outside. ..Pa Pap. ..Pa Pap. ..Pa Pap. My mouth moves with each one. The trees in New York are skeleton at this time of year, and weather forecasts are about as reliable as the stock market.

It was a harsh awakening. I didn't remember anything but the dream. I awoke on the floor, with two girls in a bed lying above me. I entered the restroom and smelled myself. They were not focused on me. Had we not confused things at all? I walked lightly back into the bedroom to see if they had died. I watched them breathe. They were fine, with a faint smile. I gathered my clothing, drank water from the kitchen sink, double-checked the bedroom, and slid out the door, which automatically locked behind me.

Last night, I saw a wave rise like a swelling balloon, and my heart sank. There are so many things I want to accomplish, I reflected as I rode in the taxi on a pleasant road, the silence returning. I wanted to peek into people's eyes several more times. Love you, I reminded myself. I adore you, too, and I followed it softly. Inside the dead of night is always the scariest place, and when you find yourself having to make a decision—scratching for safety and trying to make it to the top of Everest; turning your surfboard around and falling with every fear you've ever tried to confront down an eighty-foot mountain of water; or running from the bulls of Pamplona and you're there alone, stuck in something invisible, psychically ratcheted down—the lifesaving decision made is never the right one. That terror. The paralyzing terror. Fear has bullied me my entire life. I love you. I really love you. That terror has always attempted to kill me. It tormented me. "Total commitment," I heard myself saying.

The cabbie looked over his shoulder and asked, "What was that?"

"Nothing. Sorry. "Nothing," I barely responded.

I got up, listened to the pigeons, and went outside. There was always another step to look forward to. Perhaps something like this has always existed.

2022

Our daughter responds to our efforts to establish stronger boundaries. So does our other daughter. Today, however, at the playground, there was a complete meltdown, and we were not having it. She wailed in my arms the entire way to the car. I was shaking as I closed the car door. In such a situation, she demands an unprecedented level of attention. I knelt, unsure what to do. And while I pacified her, I knew that whatever she was feeling would come out eventually.

I got back in the car while Kathryn was chatting to her. I was sweaty, unsure, and exposed. It took two hours to get coffee this morning. I was frayed. I'm fat. I am not a good father. Everything was running through my thoughts.

I quickly jumped out of the car and began walking. Home was roughly a mile and a half distant. I was making it about myself.

She pulled up alongside me.

"Get in."

"No."

"Get IN."

"I cannot do this!"

She then drove away, reappearing approximately halfway through, this time with a bottle of water.

"Here. "At least take this."

"I do not want it! Can I take a moment? Only one?!? Leave. Simply drive home. Thank you."

I craved the water the moment she pulled away. It's quite humid here. The air lands on you. It does not simply blow by like in the desert. Southern air is like invisible molasses. My jeans are soaked, and my shirt is a different hue now. I'm sore from trying to get my body back into shape. I am a baby. I do not deserve all these presents.

I was almost home when I noticed a silver Mercedes-Benz pulled aside.

"Excuse me."

A middle-aged woman with dark hair done in a southern style and thick red lipstick glanced at me, something between afraid and smiling.

"The Lord told me to turn around," she explained. "I see you. Are you OK? Do you need prayer?"

I stared at her as if she had been sent to me. I wondered if this happened all the time here or if it was just me, her, and the kids, plus the fact that I've made a career out of seeming angry.

"I apologize?"

"Do you know Jesus Christ?"

I thought about it.

Yes, I do. I am aware of him. I see him in my imagination and occasionally in my heart. I liked who he was. What he represented. He hung out with beggars and prostitutes. He encouraged the outcast to feel entire. He resembled Jim Jones, but he wasn't looking to make amends. As far as we can tell, he wasn't motivated by power. Oh, and allegedly he was God's son.

"Yes, I know him. Thank you," and I walked away.

As I started my journey home, I reflected on the miracle I had just rejected. Why didn't I grasp her hand and pray with her? What could it have hurt?

How could she realize I was in pain?

Years ago, while I was working in the Bahamas, a woman approached me in a grocery shop and said, "You have sad eyes. You have the saddest eyes I've ever seen." She then walked away.

That was a moment I'd never forget.

It's stuck with me ever since.

2023

I SHOULD HAVE TAKEN EVERYTHING, I thought to myself. Cormac had died only a few days before, and here I was alone in the center of his house, searching over everything he had left behind. I looked at the pool table we had never played. I would read the bookcases as he sat on the far couch in front of the fire, nursing a steak and onions cooked by his son John, while I asked him which authors he liked best: "I don't know. Ugh. "I don't know," he'd say with distaste. To my right were two large paintings of the same parrot. His typewriter, on which he had written the last twenty-five or thirty years of books, was at the foot of his bed, behind me and to the right, sitting sadly on a carved-out piece of wood to keep it steady on his mattress.

I asked Cormac to sign my typewriter a few years back. A weak moment. A human moment. "Oh, no. Why? If I sign yours, I'll have to sign others." I felt humiliated, and rightfully so. I was prioritizing my relationship with him over our friendship. It did not make any sense. I understand now. It was a request that trivialized the friendship. Allow collectors to pay top cash for some soiled underpants that may contain the atoms of genius. Allow them to take it in their hands, bring it up to their faces, and rub the magic into their pores. Let them do it.

On one of those days, after helping him take deluded sips of Diet Coke the night before he died, I strolled into his wardrobe and found a pair of his boots. I stood there and stared down at them, remembering our chats about Sam Shepard and how, despite their friendship, Cormac had never read a single word of his writing. There were also hanging the tweed sport jackets he was known to wear frequently: nice clothes or, more likely, clothes he could afford at the time. Then there's the culturally appropriate safe in the closet, which probably contains a couple rifles and handguns. I did not attempt to open the safe. The majority of the remaining apparel was wrapped in plastic after it had been dry cleaned.

I remembered when I walked into my mother's closet at the ranch the day following her death. I pressed her sweatshirt against my face, but any traces of her were already gone. This felt similar. Cormac was gone. I was going to miss him.

Less than a year later, there was an auction. His desk, which he had constructed from cherry wood in Tennessee years ago, was for sale. The desk started at fifteen thousand dollars. An emotion came over me: "I should have that desk," I heard myself exclaim. If I had that desk, my writing might improve. Then the infection spread. I imagined myself wandering around his house alone. Cormac's place. His house of 25 years. His refuge, whatever that was to him. I was torn between a friend at a loss and a scoundrel.

He was just a man. He told me he didn't know why he wrote the way he did. I simply sit down, it arrives, and I type it. Is it necessary to give a reason? I'm not sure what it is. "I don't care." There was the work, and there were others who responded to it. That is it. I've realized you're a genius and a disaster of an artist are near cousins.

The hollow desire that swept through me was followed by shame. How could I be so human and so mediocre. "I should've taken a bunch of shit" was all that felt like: the tweed coats, cowboy boots, knickknacks, paper, books, dirt, and trash. And I felt ashamed because I knew I wasn't doing it to protect my pal. It was because, like everyone else, I was looking for validation. "These are Cormac's undergarments. I rub it into my face. Will you rub it in yours? "Let us be ordinary together."

It's difficult to be weak—human, whatever you call it. It's embarrassing as hell.

1976/1995/2021

BIRDS ARE CHIRPING WILDLY OUTSIDE. My small, tight office window is cracked open to let some cold air in because the blasting heater blowing right against my thighs from under the desk won't stop.

Last night, we went through my mother's old cookbooks, which are stacked beside me. Kathryn wants to prepare one of her recipes. There are reams of recipes, all in her handwriting and written on a restaurant's personal notepads, napkins, or any scrap of paper she could find. Every restaurant she visited, she would wind up in the kitchen, asking a slew of questions about how they made their food differently than she did, or what new dishes they were preparing that she could personalize at home (and certainly improve on). She would make herself known. She couldn't control herself. And those old handwritten recipes remind me of our days on the road, conversing on the CB to stray truckers who we'd eventually meet at an agreed-upon truck stop somewhere along whichever route we were on. Those eighteen-wheeler Peterbilts, Macks, and Kenworths are framed by Christmasy parking lights shimmering against a howling desert wind, and in the background, those big truckers visible through the large-paned window sit on stools against the wraparound counter, all their snap button-down dirty white shirts and heavily calloused oil-stained fingers resting on tins of Copenhagen or packs of Pall Mall cigarettes.

All of the waiters in these establishments were prune-skinned women who had spent their entire lives caring for men like these. They smiled a lot, trying to make an extra twenty or thirty cents on what might only be a half-smile back.

And there'd she be, my mom, walking in there, me shuffling at her side, replete with Bruce Lee T-shirt and jeans frayed below my pair of semi worn cowboy boots clicking on the parking lot asphalt; and all the men would look up to her three-hundred-pound voice they had come to know through those CB lines, and there she'd be, all 105 pounds of her, rhinestone and leather fringed: the ready-made blonde raring to go and readily bellowing, "Which one goes by the handle 'Cowboy'"and that man would slowly raise a smeared hand, as if someone had just run over it and he'd reply in a voice almost as deep as hers:" Yes, ma'am. That would be me." The waves would part as she walked into that truckers' refuge, that tilted-mirror pie-displaying oasis.

They called her Cat Lady. It was because she managed a rescue station for wild creatures in distress. It was a suitable handle.

All animal people are insane. All of them. Dog lovers aren't animal people. People who send their tough-as-nails ranch workers in with a full-grown untrained lion that eventually sinks its teeth into one of their thighs and your mother laughs so hard she nearly can't say

"Well, you better get outta there" are animal people, and they're batshit nuts. I grew up with them. They raised me, and I understand them, thankfully or not.

Truckers are as close to human animals as it gets. They are feral and act on instinct. Given that, they were the demographic my mother could secure because she was an outsider to everyone else. People outside of the trucker social club adored her, but after a while they realized they were swimming with a shark: an abnormality, a challenge. Everyone wants to swim with sharks every now and then because it makes them feel like they're one of the selected few who were intended to live. They might even want to return and try it. As a result, people would get bitten and depart repeatedly.

Cooking, however, was one thing she could do effortlessly. She'd place food on people's fence posts at the start of their dirt roads, and they'd wave back the next day as she drove me to school. She'd help start tiny, local restaurants in the neighborhood before discussing the possibility of opening her own. The night she died, she even stocked the refrigerator with six dessert dishes. Three days later, when we hosted a gathering at the ranch to remember her, that's what everyone ate: her sweet creations, the only sweet she had. My mother moved indoors. Even after she'd died.

So, from these strewn pieces of recipe ingredients comes a history. And with that chicken scratch history, my wife will try to bring it back to life with our tiny kids.

She will always be somewhere.

She refuses to disappear.

Jane's constant appearance.

2018

THERE IT WAS AGAIN, THAT SILENCE. He'd walked all day

with his pockets full of phrases and letter shavings he'd collected during the previous few days. He had been thinking a lot, and the thoughts were loud, but now it was silent. He'd whittled away fragments and stored them in his pockets to work out later, when the machine wasn't so hot. But, for the time being, he became silent as he paused along the edge of the cliff overlooking the sea, took all the jagged would-be phrases in his hands, and scattered them on the dusty ground beneath him. It was early in the morning inside a foggy marine front, and he could hear seagulls panting overhead to the north, but he didn't try to listen to them.

To the west, the onshore breeze was strong enough to whip the rabbit ears of his inside-out pockets, but he couldn't feel them, or himself.

And while he stared down at all those broken thoughts, he kept preventing himself from putting together a logical statement, from structuring what the architecture of that breeze desired to do, since it wasn't right yet. Nothing was fitting together intuitively. No, he stood there with his head down, staring at the potpourri. He observed it as if he were standing at his grandfather's bedside, knowing that there would soon be no more words from his pruned mouth; quiet but for these ludicrous brushstrokes of life shriveling. He reached down, picked up the grunt or moan he remembered hearing, and began again. He felt a nice breeze and imagined the smoke from his mother's Kool Kings being sucked out her driver's side window. Then he sat down on the dirt and continued shuffling the noises until he reached: "The child's laughing shook him so violently that he couldn't help but chuckle. He lifted her onto his shoulders, her hands entwined over his forehead, and they strolled to the ice cream shop for some soft serve—half chocolate, half vanilla—her mouth nibbling at his short hair from above as they went. ."When he looked up, saw another seagull pass above him, heard the breakwater below, and felt it all, he went straight back into it, slowly, word by newborn word.

2023

(Reema)

SHE MADE IT SO SHE COULD TRAVEL. While traveling, she could see what other people did and did, which matched her interests. It could have come from how she grew up. It could have had anything to do with her stepfather, Seth.

Regardless, as a child, she was captivated by why people did what they did, so she made it her profession—a photographer, a writer, a journalist—whatever would put her at the forefront of that anthill of mankind.

She eventually navigated her way around the world. In Sri Lanka, she observed a Russian tattoo being buzzed onto the thick skin of an elderly guy with virtually no room left on his body for additional art, and she inquired about the history of his so-visible journal; he told her because she was interested, and she listened closely. She went to a new rehabilitation program in the Netherlands and talked to the patients about the brain and chemistry, and what birds do when they get bored. She then checked herself in as an experiment and learned a lot about choices and how the word freedom can also have hiding places. She ran with a little hustler in Rome and helped pickpocket obese tourists or anyone with a camera strap around their neck, and she sweated uncontrollably with some of the Native Americans in the red hills of New Mexico, seeing visions of animals she had never seen before but later discovered to be real. She raced with both devils and angels, and most of the time she couldn't tell them apart. The more she traveled and experienced, the more she realized how interconnected the globe was. Africa had a special effect on her as she writhed on the ground, parasites assaulting her viscera. Young children came to her relief, applying pastes to her forehead and placing their hands on her stomach like a casket. She can still feel their tiny hands on her stomach, which relieved much of the discomfort.

There was surfing in Australia with the wild and whimsical, gray-bearded Barton Lynch, and that shark encounter; then there was the film set in Wadi Rum, Jordan, where she spent three nights in the glass globe out in the middle of the desert sands and spoke to someone who didn't speak English about the constellation of stars above them and what it meant to the ancients. She learnt, and with each experience, she became less knowledgeable.

After years of travel, she sat down one day to write a book on the people she had met and what she had learnt. With a #2 pencil in hand, she began to write:

We now see each other for flaws and wounds. There is no more hiding. It is a total exposure. However, the mystery remains since we are all changing every day: each decision, reaction to someone, necessity, and desire manifested on one platform or another. We are exposed to a lot of information that is overwhelming and encompassing. I'm grateful for everything, including the diarrhea and diamonds. It is a vibrant, heated era, and our time here is limited and valuable. What will characterize us this year? How shall we treat one another? We are responsible for our own fates. People will embarrass you in passing, just as they did in school; or, in turn, you may be the shamer, that puffed-up bully who shoulder checks the smaller version of yourself simply to feel more conspicuous and prepared. However, you will suffer as well, because the law of averages will always catch up with you. So be yourself, but try to be kind whenever possible. Honor any gifts you may have. Sing loudly in the shower or send a lovely letter to your grandmother. We are in a truly fortunate situation. We are lucky as a species to have anything at all.

Reema slumped over her words, rereading them several times. She enjoyed what it said and where it came from, but it didn't credit everything that was inside her. It read more like a letter to a dear friend she wanted to unload on than a novel. She put down her pencil and strolled out of her hotel room to look out over the Red Sea, where she noticed a small boat just lifting its sail. She watched as it filled with the same wind she could feel ruffling the back of her head, giving the impression that she had something to do with what would eventually propel that boat out into the ocean. She knew she'd stop writing because she couldn't make sense of the title.

People were kind to her, she told herself, and she was kind to them. Everything was shared: a bit here, a little there.

The sea reminds me of her. Years have gone, and every time I go away—in the desert, in the mountains—I feel that craving for the sea's, albeit absurd, unpredictability. She holds my mother's ashes after we scattered them into the river that crosses our property on the Central Coast, eventually leading to where we all came from: the sea. We wondered if her ashes might make their way into the potable water of all the local wells, causing everyone with the Crazy Jane bullfrogs to croak, at least for a day or two: traces of what once was. It made us laugh. We longed, in our stupid and hungry ways, to hear her voice one final time, despite its assaultive basis. She was funny. She was unusual. She was everything most people are scared of today: different, not as an affectation, but as a mineral. I see her in my children, in the way they emphasize a point or find awe in what would otherwise appear banal, but in ways that are less harmful and more peaceful. Imagine my mother in peace.

Recently, many Super 8 reels of her running around as a tiny kid were revealed. To see my mother as a tiny girl perplexed me; in my mind, she has always been a powerful adult. And when I watched those scratchy, fading colors with her laughing as she ran around, I looked to my left and right to see my small children doing the same thing with identical smiles and glints of mischief in their eyes. I like it. It moves me to know that they have inside them the freedom she sought. Her lack of grace in that freedom drove her nuts, or nearly so. I don't see that in my children.

There's so much to write. There are many stories to tell. I guess I'm looking for a greater meaning underneath it all. That world was massive, and it is now more literal. I haven't decided which I like.

The contents of this book may not be copied, reproduced or transmitted without the express written permission of the author or publisher. Under no circumstances will the publisher or author be responsible or liable for any damages, compensation or monetary loss arising from the information contained in this book, whether directly or indirectly. .

Disclaimer Notice:

Although the author and publisher have made every effort to ensure the accuracy and completeness of the content, they do not, however, make any representations or warranties as to the accuracy, completeness, or reliability of the content. , suitability or availability of the information, products, services or related graphics contained in the book for any purpose. Readers are solely responsible for their use of the information contained in this book

Every effort has been made to make this book possible. If any omission or error has occurred unintentionally, the author and publisher will be happy to acknowledge it in upcoming versions.

Copyright © 2024

All rights reserved.

Printed in Great Britain
by Amazon